Preceding page shows the Hadassah Hospital in Jerusalem.

BY BEATRICE BOISH AND MARY JANE ZUKIN

from noodles to strudels

ART BY LEONA HERTZBERG AND JOE JOYCE

First Printing 1972
Second Printing 1974
Third Printing 1975
Fourth Printing 1977
Fifth Printing 1978

Copyright © 1972 by Beverly Hills Chapter of Hadassah
Library of Congress Card No. 72-92793

Printed in the United States of America

THIS BOOK IS PUBLISHED IN THE 60TH ANNIVERSARY YEAR OF HADASSAH, the Women's Zionist Organization of America, by the women of Beverly Hills Chapter of Hadassah. From its inception, the women of Hadassah have made of volunteerism a crown of pride and accomplishment. While other women are demonstrating, Hadassah women are doing.

AS AN AMERICAN-BASED ORGANIZATION of over 325,000 members, Hadassah conducts a vast education program. It has helped administer countless such programs as President Kennedy's "Food for Peace", as well as community efforts to eliminate hunger in this abundant land.

AS A ZIONIST ORGANIZATION, Hadassah has the upbuilding of the State of Israel as a primary function. Every possible need in health, education and welfare were anticipated, initiated and effected by Hadassah until the Israel Government assumed responsibility. It would require a volume larger than this to delineate all of Hadassah's accomplishments in child rescue, healing of the sick, teaching of the young, and dramatic medical research.

THE HADASSAH-HEBREW UNIVERSITY MEDICAL CENTER, pictured on the end sheets of this book, is the source of remarkable research in all fields including Nutrition. The Hadassah Community College and the Comprehensive High School in Jerusalem feature courses in food preparation and nutrition in their curricula. Prenatal and well-baby clinics provided by Hadassah as early as 1921 have stressed the importance of proper nutrition. A school lunch program was adopted in 1923. The Hadassah Nutrition Department was not taken over by the Israel Government until 1950. The Hadassah Hospital atop Mount Scopus, unoccupied from 1948 until 1967, will reopen its doors in 1974 following complete rebuilding. It will house the finest, most modern health facilities. Hadassah serves all who come--Moslem, Christian, Jew. Its staffs are composed of people of all faiths from over seventy nations working together in paths of peace.

PROCEEDS FROM "NOODLES TO STRUDELS" will go to maintain all the above projects. Its many contributors and the co-editors, Mesdames Jerome Boish and Paul Zukin will be rewarded by its success. Mrs. Jack Lasman, immediate past Chapter President, during whose administration this work was begun and with whose constant encouragement it was completed, deserves a special word of appreciation.

"Go thy way, eat thy bread with joy and drink with a merry heart."
(Ecclesiastes)

Mrs. Howard Landres
President, Beverly Hills Chapter
of Hadassah

September 1972

Mary Jane Zukin graduated from UCLA with a degree in dietetics and has attended graduate courses in nutrition at the UCLA School of Public Health. She has worked as a quality control chemist and has taught home economics and nutrition at the high school level. In the late 1960's Mary Jane served as a consultant to the Greek Government developing handicrafts on the island of Crete. She is presently teaching nutrition to low income mothers in a clinic of the Los Angeles Health Department.

****

Beatrice Boish is a former New Yorker, and a graduate of the New York Institute of Dietetics. She received her hospital training at Community Hospital (formerly Madison Park) in Brooklyn. She has successfully catered many charitable luncheons and teas. In 1971 as a member of New Life Auxiliary for Cerebral Palsy she entered the Lawry Foods Inc. Contest. She was a Lawry's cook off participant, and received a trophy for the Geoff Edwards KMPC favorite recipe award.

We have devoted two years to collecting recipes from members of the Beverly Hills Chapter of Hadassah. We carefully tested each recipe in our own homes for accuracy and quality. Sometimes, after testing, we combined similar recipes. In some cases we have substituted non-dairy margarine and non-dairy creamers and soups in order to observe the Jewish dietary laws. If you can't find your recipe, don't fret. We ran out of time, and yours will appear in our next edition.

We could never have produced this book without the many people who helped us.

After the recipes were checked out of our kitchens, Joan Kheel and La Verne Provisor reviewed each one insuring that the instructions would be accurate and easy to follow. They also proof read the book for spelling and typing errors.

The drawings brought the book to life by adding sparkle and charm. For this, we thank Leona Hertzberg. Leona also helped do the lay-outs for the book.

Joe Joyce, our honorary member, stood behind us guiding every step. In addition, he designed the cover and lettered the section guides.

Loraine Goldbloom and Dudley Gordon gave the book a professional touch by hand lettering the titles.

Every project benefits by having someone who will step in to help where ever needed. Rae Siegel was our "girl Friday". We thank her for all the help she gave us.

Our typists were essential to the printing of this book. They per-formed beyond the call of duty. We have listed their names separately on Page 7.

We thank each one of you who contributed recipes. We realize that many of you made sacrifices by contributing long treasured family secrets.

A very special thanks to our families. Our husbands, Jerry Boish and Paul Zukin, were long-suffering and patient. Lena Zukin acted as technical consultant. Benjamin, Louis, and Jerry Boish helped with the testing and contributed some of their cherished recipes. Mary Jane's children, Barbara, James H., and Donald, helped in countless ways.

Mary Jane Zukin
Dietician

Beatrice Boish
Dietician

There's many a gal I have seen
To whom cooking was reason to scream
              And then took a look
              Inside of this book
And now finds cooking a dream.

```
Co-Editors. . . . . . . . . . . . . . . . . . . Joan Kheel
                                        La Verne Provisor

Assistant Editor. . . . . . . . . . . . . . . Rae Siegel

Lettering . . . . . . . . . . . . . . . .Loraine Goldbloom
                                          Dudley Gordon


        Typists:

                Jessie Barge
                Georgeanne Block
                Esther Cooper
                Marilyn Flekman
                Lottie Kluner
                Susan Squire
                Esther Walters
                Edythe Wolff*


*Over and beyond the call of duty.
```

CHERISHED RECIPES CONTRIBUTED BY WOMEN WHO CARE

DOROTHY ALTSHULER
FRAN ASH
MARTHA ARTZT
ANN BALL
JESSIE BARGE
VI BARKER
RUTH BART
ESTHER BELOUS
LESLIE BENBASSAT
DOROTHY BERKOWITZ
EUNICE BERMAN
FRANCES BLANC
JUDY BLECKMAN
GEORGEANNE BLOCK
NATALIE BLOCK
ALICE BLOOM
BERT BLOOM
SHIRLEY BLUMENTHAL
MERNA BORSTEIN
CLARA BRANDES
JUNE BROTT
PHOEBE BRYAN
SUSAN BRYAN
MARGO CARREY
CYMA COHEN
JOYCE COHEN
ROSEMARY COOPER
CHARLOTTE CRAMER
LILLIAN CZACKO

FLORENCE DAPEER
BEA DAVID
EDITH DAVIDSON
SELMA DAYE
JUNE DECKMAN
BARBARA DELMAN
THELMA DESSER
ROSE DICKENS
JOAN DREIFUS
MARCIA DUBIN
JUNE EHRLICH
MILLIE EILENBERG
BETTY ESHELMAN
SYLVIA FEINGOLD
ROSLYN FIELD
ANITA FIELDS
JAYNE FINK
EDDY FISHBEIN
DOROTHY FRISS
FAN GALPERSON
ANNE GOLDENBERG
MERALEE GOLDMAN
TILLY GOLDSTONE
RHEE GOODMAN
CLAIRE GORDON
DOROTHY GOULD
LIZ GOULD
BUNNE GREENSPAHN*
BARBARA GREENSPAN

*Deceased

MARILYN GROSS
CLARE HARMS
ESTHER HARRIS
HANK HARRIS
CHARLOTTE HART
JUDY HARTE
RUTH HELFMAN
LILLIAN HERMAN
DIANNE HERSCHER
LEONA HERTZBERG
PAULINE HIRSH
MILDRED HIRSON
CARRIE HODES
LAURIE HOOVER
KATE JACKMAN
LOLA JACKMAN
MARJORIE JOSEPH
ROSE JOSEPHSON
MILLICENT JOYCE
HELENA KANE
MOLLIE KAPLAN
SADIE KAPLAN
BARBARA KHEEL
JOAN KHEEL
SHIRLEY KIRSCH
FREDA KLEINMAN
IRENE KLINE
FREDA KURTZMAN
LILLIAN LAFF
MIMI LANDRES
MARGOT LANGFUS
TERRI LANGFUS
LUCILLE LASAROW
RUTH LASMAN
MYRA LAX
CLAUDIA LESTER
HELEN LEVINE
EDITH LEVENDORF
CHARLOTTE LEVINE
JESSIE LEVY
BERNICE LEWIS
JOYCE LEYTUS
ETHEL LOZABNICK
CELE MARSHALL
MARILYN MARTIN
LUCILLE MELCHER
CORRINE MILLER
MOLLIE MILLER

PEARL MILLER
CAROLE OKEN
ROSE OS
HORTENSE PERLER
SHIRLEY POLLACK
LA VERNE PROVISOR
LILLIAN PRUSAN
MILLIE RATNER
GLORIA REISER
THELMA ROGELL
BEA ROSE
BESS ROSENBERG
LILY ROSMAN
EVA ROTH
WYNNE ROTHBAUM
GRETA ROY
CLARA RUBIN
CLARE SATNICK
FLORENCE SCHNEIDER
VIVIAN SCHNEIDER
JUNE SCHORIN
SUZANNE SCHWARTZ
CLARA SHAPIRO
ETTA SHAPIRO
MARION SHINBANE
EVELYN SIDNEY
ESTHER SIEGEL
RAE SIEGEL
ROSE SLOBODIN
DINAH SMITH
DEBBIE SNYDER
BERNICE SPITZER
FRANCES STAWISKY
ADELE STEINBERG
EVELYN STERES
SELMA STULMAN
RUTH SWERDLOW
BONNIE TASH
URSULA TENBRINK
LILLIAN WARNER
BLOSSOM WEINER
HARRIET WHITE
JUDY WILKIN
SHIRLEY WOLPA
SARA YOUSEM
REVA ZEIGER
TONI ZIMON
LENA ZUKIN

COOKING INSTRUCTIONS

All margarine used in the recipes indicate the non-dairy variety.

Dairy products (whipping cream, sour cream, cream, and butter) may always be substituted for their non-dairy equivalents; however the resulting dish may no longer be acceptable under the Jewish dietary laws.

The flour used is always "all purpose" unless otherwise stated.

Tuna must be washed, drained, and flaked in all recipes. All recipes were tested with solid water pack white albacore tuna.

Gelatin recipes that state "whip gelatin" should only be whipped until slightly fluffy. Over-whipping will result in a product that will not stand up when unmolded.

Broth or stock may be substituted with 1 cup of water and 1 bouillon cube for each cup of broth or stock called for in the recipe.

We have salted lightly to protect your arteries, but you may add more salt if desired.

Do not use a pan that has ever been greased if an "ungreased angel pan" is called for.

Confectioners' sugar, powdered sugar, and frosting sugar are interchangeable.

In testing this book, no granulated brown sugar was used.

TABLE OF CONTENTS

The recipes in this book were made using the following equivalents:

> 1/2 lemon equals 2 tablespoons
> 1 orange equals 1/2 cup
> 1 lb. butter equals 2 cups
> 4 tablespoons butter equals 1/4 cup

One standard measuring cup at the 8 oz. mark holds the following measures:

> 8 oz. of liquids or shortening
> 5 oz. of flour
> 7 oz. of sugar
> 3 oz. of grated nuts
> 3 oz. of grated cheese

The following chart has been included so you may still use this book when the country converts to the metric system.

> 1/4 cup = 1/20 liter
> 1/2 cup = 1/10 liter plus 6 grams
> 1   cup = 1/4 liter minus 25 grams

CORN
MEAL
>   2/3 cup = 100 grams
> 1-1/8 cup = 150 grams
> 1-3/4 cup = 250 grams

COCOA   5/8 cup = 100 grams

SUGAR   7/8 cup = 200 grams
> 1 cup plus 1 tablespoon = 250 grams

BUTTER 2 tablespoons = 25 grams
> 4 tablespoons = 50 grams
> 6 tablespoons = 75 grams

from canapes to Knishes

EPICUREAN MELANGE

A gourmet appetizer for weddings

        brains--1 lb.
        sweetbreads--1 pair
        lemon juice--1 tablespoon
        flour--4 tablespoons
        salt--1/2 teaspoon
        pepper--1/8 teaspoon
        beef broth--1 cup
        margarine--4 tablespoons
        onions--1 cup, minced
        fresh mushrooms--1/2 lb., sliced
        non-dairy creamer--1 cup

Soak brains and sweetbreads in cold water for 20 minutes. Remove all membranes. Place in pot. Add fresh water to cover. Measure water. Add a teaspoon of salt to each quart of water. Add lemon juice. Simmer uncovered for 20 minutes.

Drain well. Cut into bite size pieces. Set aside. Mix non-dairy creamer, flour, salt, and pepper into beef broth. Set aside. Melt margarine in a heavy skillet. Cook onions until golden brown. Add mushrooms. Saute 2 minutes. Mix thoroughly. Add broth mixture. Blend well. Stir until thick. Add sweetbreads and heat through, about 5 minutes.

Serve on patty shell as a first course. Serves 10.

SPINACH KNISHES

A Middle East delicacy

    frozen spinach--30 oz., chopped and drained
    Mozzarella cheese--12 oz., cut into 1/2" cubes
    Parmesan cheese--1 cup, grated
    unsalted butter--4 tablespoons, hard, cut into pieces
    green onions--1/2 cup, minced
    salt--1/2 teaspoon
    pepper--1/16 teaspoon
    filo dough--18 sheets
    melted butter--1-1/2 cups
    bread crumbs--2 cups

Mix spinach, cheeses, butter, onions, salt, and pepper together. Brush 6 leaves of filo dough with melted butter. Sprinkle bread crumbs over each leaf. Lay one leaf on top of the other making a stack of six leaves.

Spoon 1/3 of spinach filling along long edge of stack. Roll up like a jelly roll.

Make two more rolls using up filo dough and spinach filling.

Place on baking sheet with seam side down. Brush with more butter. Bake at 325°F for 35 minutes. Increase temperature to 400°F to brown, about 5 minutes.

Cut on diagonal to make about 45 pieces. Serve hot.

"A feast is made for laughter, and wine maketh glad the life." (Ecclesiastes.)

OPEN SESAMES

Nice with drinks, hard or soft

sesame seeds--1/2 cup, hulled
butter--4 tablespoons
flour--1 cup
salt--1/2 teaspoon
pepper--1/8 teaspoon
cheddar cheese--1/2 cup, grated
milk--1 tablespoon

Brown sesame seeds at 450°F for 5 minutes, until brown. Mix
other ingredients and blend as for pastry dough. Sprinkle
bread board with half of the browned seeds. Roll dough thin
and cover top with remaining seeds. Roll over with pin to
secure seeds. Cut in strips 1" wide and bake at 300°F for
7 minutes, until lightly brown. Re-heat to crisp before
serving. (Hulled sesame seeds will be found in a health food
store.)

GARDEN AND GRAVY

Raw vegetables and dip

    whipped cottage cheese--1 pint (or sour cream)
    white horseradish--1-1/3 tablespoons
    paprika--1 teaspoon
    minced chives--1 teaspoon
    salt--1 teaspoon
    tarragon--1 teaspoon
    monosodium glutamate--1/4 teaspoon
    garlic--1 clove, crushed
    pepper--1/8 teaspoon

Blend well and allow to ripen in refrigerator overnight.

Use as a dip for the following raw vegetables: carrot sticks, radish roses, celery sticks, raw cauliflowerettes, cucumber sticks, and thin turnip slices.

LAZY DAY VEGETABLE DIP

    whipped cottage cheese--1 pint
    curry powder--1 tablespoon

Mix and serve with raw vegetables. Good and easy too.

STUFFED MUSHROOMS

I could eat all of these by myself

    fresh mushrooms--1/2 lb. (1" to 1-1/2" in diameter)
    mayonnaise--6 tablespoons
    sour cream--6 tablespoons
    chopped chives--1/4 cup
    paprika--1/2 teaspoon

Clean mushrooms with a washcloth. Remove stems. Place caps concave side up in a square pan or pie tin. Chop stems. Mix stems with mayonnaise, sour cream, and chives. Stuff mushrooms with this mixture. Sprinkle paprika over tops. Bake at 350°F for 30 minutes. Serve as a hot hors d'oeuvre. These can be prepared the day before and baked just before using.

Makes about 20.

GRANDMOTHER'S HERRING

I'm the grandmother who is making this now

        fat herring fillets--1 quart
        sour cream--1 pint (2 cups)
        sugar--1/2 cup
        oranges--2, sliced
        lemons--2, sliced
        Bermuda onion--1 large, sliced

Drain liquid from herring. Add sour cream and sugar. Set
aside a few fruit slices for decoration, then add rest of
fruit and the onions to the herring. Cover tightly and let
marinate for a few hours before serving. Serves 20.

ANTIPASTO SOL

Something extra for company barbecue

        tuna--2 cans (7 oz. each)
        olive oil--1/4 cup
        cider vinegar--2 tablespoons
        tomato sauce--8 oz. can
        cocktail onions--2 oz. jar
        gherkin pickles--3 oz., halved
        sliced pimento--2 oz. jar
        black pitted olives--10 oz. can
        green pitted olives--10 oz. can
        artichoke hearts--2 small jars (6 oz. each)
        fresh mushrooms--1/4 lb., cleaned and sliced

Drain and mix all ingredients together and marinate 24 hours
before serving. Place large lettuce leaves around edge of
salad bowl. Spoon antipasto in middle. Let guests help
themselves.

LOX PINWHEELS

Colorful hors d'oeuvres

    lox--1/2 lb.
    whipped cream cheese--4 oz.
    chives--1 teaspoon
    miniature bagels--one dozen, split and buttered

Mix cream cheese and chives. Spread mixture over lox. Roll
up like a jelly roll. Wrap tightly in wax paper. Refrigerate at least 4 hours. Slice crosswise to give pinwheel
effect.

Serve on bagels.

SWEET AND SOUR FISH

This tastes very much like old-fashioned herring

        water--2 cups
        allspice--1-1/2 teaspoons
        white vinegar--1 cup
        sugar--1 cup
        salt--1 teaspoon
        white fish--3 lbs., cut into 6 pieces
        white onions--2 large, sliced thin

Mix water with seasonings, sugar, and salt. Add fish and
onions and simmer until just tender. It will toughen if
overcooked. My slices took 5 minutes to cook. Put fish into a bottle and cover with cooking liquid. Screw cover on
tightly. Chill in refrigerator for 3 days. Serve as an
appetizer for 16.

GREEK BOREK

Cheese appetizers just like we had in Greece

    parsley--1/2 cup, chopped
    feta or Greek cheese--1 lb.
    pot cheese--12 oz.
    eggs--5 large
    butter--1 cup, melted
    strudel dough--1 lb. (ask for filo dough)

Mix parsley, cheese and eggs together.

Melt butter. Cut dough into 60 three inch strips. Keep
covered with a damp cloth until used. Take out one strip.
Place on waxed paper. Brush with butter. Put a teaspoon of
cheese at one end. Fold end of dough over cheese forming a
triangle. Continue folding and turning to end being careful
to keep triangle shape. You will now have completely
wrapped the cheese in dough. Continue until you have used
up all of the cheese. Bake on a cookie sheet at 425°F for
15 to 20 minutes or until golden brown. These may be served
cold, but I like them hot. Makes about 60 turnovers.

CHOPPED LIVER

You'll get hugged for this one

    beef liver--2 lbs., skinned and de-veined
    onions--2 medium, diced
    oil--1/2 cup
    seasoned salt--1-1/2 teaspoon
    black pepper--1/2 teaspoon
    mayonnaise--3 tablespoons
    eggs--6 extra large, hard cooked
    egg bread (challah)--2 slices
    garlic powder--1/8 teaspoon

Put diced onions and oil into a large skillet. Fry until
tender and golden, but not brown. Add liver, which has been
cut in small pieces. Cook only until liver is no longer
pink. Put liver, onions, and pan juices through grinder.
Then grind the eggs and lastly the bread. Mix all ingredients well. Add salt, pepper, garlic, and mayonnaise.

Do not freeze.

SALMON PATE

salmon--7-3/4 oz. can
cream cheese--5 oz., softened
lemon juice--1 tablespoon
onion--2 tablespoons, grated
horseradish--1 teaspoon
liquid smoke--1/4 teaspoon
chopped pecans--1/2 cup
parsley--1/2 cup, chopped

Flake salmon, removing bones and skin. Mix with the cheese,
lemon, onion, horseradish, and liquid smoke. Press into
ball. Chill several hours. Roll in nuts and parsley before
serving. Serve with crackers.

PARTY FRANKS

These are so good you'll need a double batch

cocktail franks--1 lb., or
hot dogs--1 lb., cut in thirds
non-dairy sour cream--1/2 pint (1 cup)
mustard--4 tablespoons, prepared
ketchup--1/4 cup
garlic salt--1/4 teaspoon

Put cocktail franks in a pan of water. Cook until done.
Mix other ingredients thoroughly. Heat. Fill bottom of
chafing dish with boiling hot water. Place cooked, heated
cocktail franks in chafing dish and pour heated sauce over.

Serves 8.

EASY HORS D'OEUVRES

A party dish with little work

cocktail franks--2 lbs. (or standard size hot
                         dogs cut in thirds)
ketchup--14 oz. bottle
grape jelly--10 oz. jar

Mix ketchup and jelly together. Heat and stir to blend
well. Simmer franks in hot sauce 5 minutes. Keep warm in
chafing dish. Serve with toothpicks. Serves 20.

QUEEN'S HERRING

```
    fat fillet of herring--2 lb. jar, drained
    onions--2 small
    challah or egg bread--3 slices
    apples--3 large, peeled and cored
    eggs--4 large, hard cooked
```

Rinse fillets in a colander. Put all ingredients in food grinder. Mix thoroughly.

Serve as appetizer with party rye.

SUNSET AWARD PATIO PIZZA

This recipe won a cash award

```
    taco chips--4 cups
    sharp cheddar cheese--1/2 lb., grated
    green chili sauce--8 oz. can
    guacamole sauce--1/2 cup (prepared)
    sour cream--1/2 cup
```

Spread chips on a pizza pan. Cover with the grated cheese.
Spoon sauce evenly over chips. Put under broiler 3 to 4
minutes or until cheese melts. Watch it carefully. Remove
from oven and dot sides with guacamole and sour cream.

Serves 4, and they'll ask for more.

HERRING SALAD

Delicious with hot French bread

    herring--1 lb. jar, cut in bits, well drained
    beets--8 oz. can, chopped, drained
    apples--2 pippin, cut up
    chopped walnuts--1/2 cup
    Spanish onion--1/4 cup, chopped
    sour cream--1/4 cup

Mix all ingredients except sour cream together. Add sour
cream just before serving. To be used as an appetizer or
as a main luncheon dish.

Serves 6 to 8.

MARINATED MUSHROOMS

I seldom have guests without serving these mushrooms

        salt--1 teaspoon
        pepper--1/4 teaspoon, fresh ground
        dry mustard--1/2 teaspoon
        paprika--1/2 teaspoon
        wine vinegar--1/4 cup
        garlic--1 clove
        oil--3/4 cup
        fresh mushrooms--1/2 lb., sliced thick

Add dry ingredients to vinegar and shake well. Add garlic
and then oil. Remove garlic after several hours. Pour
dressing over mushrooms about 1 hour before serving.
Mushrooms become bitter if left in marinade overnight.
Serve with toothpicks.

You may use bottled dressing if you prefer.

MOCK KISHKE

Make your own the easy way

    celery--1 stalk, large
    carrot--1 large
    Spanish onion--1/2 medium
    margarine--1/2 cup, melted
    rich, flaky crackers--8 oz. box, crumbled

Grate or grind celery, carrot, and onion and mix with other ingredients until completely blended.

Make into 5 rolls about 7" long and 1-1/2" wide. Roll each piece in aluminum foil to retain shape. Bake for 45 minutes. Slice and serve.

MANDARIN CHICKEN WINGS

Serve at your next briss

    chicken wings--36, use meaty half
    oil--1/4 cup
    cornstarch--1 cup
    eggs--2 large
    salt--1/2 teaspoon
    monosodium glutamate--1/4 teaspoon
    garlic salt--1/8 teaspoon
    non-dairy creamer--1/4 cup
    sugar--3/4 cup
    water--1/4 cup
    vinegar--1/2 cup
    soy sauce--1 teaspoon
    ketchup--1 tablespoon

Mix together cornstarch, eggs, salt, monosodium glutamate, garlic salt, and non-dairy creamer. Dip chicken wings into mixture. Fry a few at a time in the oil until lightly browned. Combine sugar, water, vinegar, soy sauce, and ket-chup in a small saucepan and heat until sugar dissolves. Remove from heat. Dip fried chicken in sauce and place in single layers on a foil lined cookie sheet. Pour remaining sauce over chicken. Bake at 350°F for 30 minutes. Turn chicken often and watch carefully. Good as a main dish us-ing your favorite chicken parts. Serves 12.

WINGS IN CHAFING DISH

Serve these and watch them fly away

```
chicken wings--24, meaty part only
flour--6 tablespoons
salt--1/4 teaspoon
pepper--1/8 teaspoon
paprika--1/2 teaspoon
ground ginger--1/4 teaspoon
garlic--1 clove
oil--6 tablespoons
wild plum jelly--8 oz.
pineapple juice--1/2 cup
champagne vinegar--1/2 teaspoon
fresh ginger--1" x 1/8" piece, slivered
cherry tomatoes--6, cut in half
pineapple chunks--8 oz., drained
green pepper--1 medium, in chunks
green onions or shallots--1 tablespoon, minced
sesame seeds--1 teaspoon, toasted
red food coloring--2 drops
```

Turn skin down and over meat on wing so it looks like a chicken leg. Combine flour, salt, pepper, paprika, and 1/4 teaspoon ginger in a large paper bag. Place chicken in bag and shake until coated.

Place garlic clove and oil in a heavy skillet and fry chicken in hot oil until golden brown on both sides. Bake on cookie sheet in single layer at 350°F for 20 minutes.

Blend jelly, pineapple juice, vinegar, and fresh ginger in a double boiler. Heat slowly until jelly is melted and mixture is blended. Add food coloring. Mix again. It will be a bright red. Add pineapple chunks, tomato halves, green pepper chunks, and shallots. Place in chafing dish. Add chicken to chafing dish so that the bone end is sticking up. Spoon sauce over meaty part of chicken. Sprinkle with sesame seeds and serve.

****

"Spikenard and saffron, calamus and cinnamon, myrrh and aloes, with all the chief spices." (Song of Songs)

DELICIOUS KNISHES

You'll get kisses for your knishes

```
strudel dough--1/4 lb. (ask for filo dough
                    at an Italian grocery store)
creamed cottage cheese--1 lb.
butter--2 tablespoons, room temperature
salt--1/2 teaspoon
egg--1 large
potato--1 cup, mashed
butter--1/2 cup, melted
bread crumbs--1/4 cup
```

Mix cottage cheese, butter, salt, egg, and mashed potatoes together. Beat well. Butter one strudel leaf with the melted butter. Sprinkle with 1 teaspoon of crumbs. Cut into 5" squares. Place 2 tablespoons of filling in center of each square. Fold top and bottom over the center. Turn upside down and fold two sides toward center. You will now have several thicknesses of dough on both top and bottom. Continue as above until all of dough is used up. Cover with plastic until used. Place folded side down on greased cookie sheet. Prick top of each knish with a toothpick twice. Brush with butter. Bake at 325°F for 45 minutes.

Makes about 3 dozen.

QUICK SALMON MOUSSE

A beautiful mold that will please your guests

```
salmon--6 oz. can, flaked, with bones and skin removed
sour cream--1 pint (2 cups)
lemon juice--2 tablespoons
capers--2 tablespoons, if available
unflavored gelatin--2 envelopes (2 tablespoons)
non-meat dehydrated onion soup--1 to 1-1/2 oz.
boiling water--2 cups
```

Mix salmon, sour cream, lemon juice, and capers together. Dissolve gelatin and onion soup in hot water. Allow to set slightly in refrigerator. Combine with salmon mixture. Pour into well greased 1 quart mold. Chill until firm.

Unmold onto crisp lettuce leaves. Serves 6.

26

TUNA MOUSSE

This is nice to serve with crackers before dinner

        unflavored gelatin--2 oz. (2 envelopes)
        sugar--2 tablespoons
        salt--2 teaspoons
        dry mustard--1 teaspoon
        cold water--1/2 cup
        white vinegar--1/2 cup
        tuna--4 cans (7 oz. each)
        celery--2 cups, diced
        green onions--2, chopped
        whipping cream--1 cup, whipped

Mix gelatin, sugar, salt, and mustard together in top of
double boiler. Add water and vinegar. Stir until gelatin
and sugar dissolve. Chill to consistency of unbeaten egg
whites. Stir in the tuna, celery, and onion. Fold in
whipped cream. Turn into 4 cup well buttered mold. Chill
until firm. Unmold and decorate. Serves 12.

SALMON BISQUE MOUSSE

A scrumptious addition for a wedding buffet

        unflavored gelatin--2 envelopes (2 tablespoons)
        bouillon--1 cup
        salmon--3 cups, canned, drained, and flaked
        celery--1/2 cup, diced
        non-dairy sour cream--1 cup
        sherry wine--1/2 cup
        mayonnaise--1/4 cup
        sugar--1 teaspoon
        pepper--1/2 teaspoon
        onion powder--1/8 teaspoon
        salt--1/2 teaspoon
        red food coloring--2 drops
        yellow food coloring--2 drops

Soften gelatin in broth. Place over low heat and stir until
dissolved. Cool. Add other ingredients. Mix well. Pour
into well buttered 1 quart mold. By all means use a fish
mold if you have one. If your fish mold is large, double
the recipe. Unmold onto a bed of chopped parsley.

Serves 8.

OLIVE FILLED CHEESE BALLS

Everyone will have a ball

```
butter--1-1/2 tablespoons, soft
cheddar cheese--1/2 cup, grated
flour--1/4 cup
cayenne pepper--1/16 teaspoon
celery seed--1/4 teaspoon
stuffed olives--3 oz. bottle, well drained
```

Mix butter and cheese with fork until smooth. Add flour, cayenne pepper, and celery seed. Mix well. Shape 1 teaspoon of dough around each olive. Roll between palms of your hands. Place on an ungreased cookie sheet. Bake at 400°F for 15 minutes. Serve hot or cold, or store unbaked in refrigerator a day or so and bake when needed.

Makes about 1-1/2 dozen.

GUACAMOLE RING

Avocado - a California favorite

```
avocado--1-1/2 cups, mashed
sour cream--1/2 cup
onion--1 tablespoon, finely chopped
hot sauce--2 drops
unflavored gelatin--1 envelope (1 tablespoon)
water--1 cup
Italian salad dressing--1/2 cup, mixed well
```

Combine avocado, sour cream, onion, and hot sauce. Set aside. Sprinkle gelatin on 1/4 cup water in a saucepan. Stir over low heat until dissolved. Remove from heat. Add remaining water and dressing. Fold in avocado mixture.

Pour into greased 1 quart ring mold. Chill until firm. When unmolded, fill center with bean salad and surround with curly endive.

Serves 6.

28

MOTHER'S BLUEBERRY MOLD

l.g.h.

        pineapple juice--2 cups
        blueberries--16 oz. can (fruit and juice)
        sugar--2 teaspoons
        lemon gelatin--6 oz.
        sour cream--1/2 pint
        very ripe banana--1, mashed

Heat pineapple juice, 1 cup of blueberry juice, and sugar to
boiling point. Pour over gelatin and stir until dissolved.
Carefully stir in the sour cream. Beat with rotary beater
until frothy. Mix in banana. Put blueberries in bottom of
well buttered 6 cup mold; pour liquid over berries and chill
until firm.

Serves 8 to 10.

RASPBERRY MOLD

Don't let the simplicity keep you from trying this one

    raspberry gelatin--6 oz.
    boiling water--2 cups
    lemon juice--1 tablespoon
    frozen raspberries--10 oz., thawed and drained

Dissolve gelatin in boiling water. Stir thoroughly. Add
lemon juice, the juice from the berries, and water to bring
the total volume to 3-1/2 cups. Stir. Allow to set until
slightly thick. Add berries and beat until fluffy. Put into
an 8 cup greased mold. Chill until firm. Serves 10.

ORANGE FLUFF

A cool, creamy accompaniment to meat

    orange gelatin--5 pkgs. (3 oz. each)
    water and liquid from drained, crushed pineapple--6 cups
    mandarin oranges--2 cans (11 oz. each), well drained
    crushed pineapple--25 oz. can, well drained
    non-dairy whip--1 carton (10.66 fluid oz.)

Dissolve orange gelatin in boiling liquid and add drained
fruit. Put into refrigerator to thicken. Take large mixing
bowl and put into refrigerator to chill. Pour non-dairy
whip into chilled bowl; beat until thick. Pour thickened
gelatin into whipped cream and mix by hand thoroughly. Pour
into lightly greased 3 quart mold. Cover with tinfoil and
put back in refrigerator overnight. Unmold by putting mold
in lukewarm water for about 5 seconds. Serves 16.

LIME OLIVE MOLD

Serve on buffet with cold cuts

    lime gelatin--3 oz.
    boiling water--3/4 cup
    mayonnaise--1 cup
    cucumbers--1 cup, diced
    chopped onions--1 tablespoon
    chopped black olives--4-1/4 oz.

Combine mayonnaise, cucumbers, onions, and olives. Dissolve
gelatin in boiling water. Chill until slightly firm. Mix
vegetables into gelatin. Pour into 1 quart mold and chill
until firm.

TILT GELATIN MOLD

Gives a rainbow effect

red gelatin--3 oz.
fruit cocktail--16 oz. (fruit and juice)
water--1 cup

lime gelatin--3 oz.
crushed pineapple--8 oz. (fruit and juice)
water--1-1/4 cups

orange gelatin--3 oz.
mandarin oranges--11 oz., drained
water--1-1/2 cups

lemon or pineapple gelatin--6 oz.
sliced pears--16 oz. (fruit and juice)
water--2-1/2 cups

Dissolve red gelatin in 1 cup boiling water. Add fruit cocktail. Chill until slightly thickened. Pour first mixture
into a 3 quart greased mold. Place in refrigerator in a
tipped position. Use inverted saucer to keep mold in proper
position. Chill until firm.

Dissolve lime gelatin in 1-1/4 cups boiling water. Add
crushed pineapple. Chill until slightly thickened. Add
second layer. Put in refrigerator and tilt again in opposite direction.

Dissolve orange gelatin in 1-1/2 cups boiling water. Add
drained mandarin oranges. Chill until slightly thickened.
Add third layer. Put in refrigerator and tilt again in
opposite direction.

Dissolve lemon or pineapple gelatin in 2-1/2 cups boiling
water. Add sliced pears. Chill until slightly thickened.
Set mold straight for fourth flavor.

Serves 20.

ORANGE MOLD

"HADARIM" MOLD

A Hebrew word for citrus

    orange gelatin--6 oz.
    boiling water--1 cup
    orange juice--1 cup
    spiced peaches--16 oz. can (with juice)
    lemon juice--1 teaspoon
    whipped cream--8 oz.
    powdered sugar--2 tablespoons

Mix gelatin with boiling water. Stir until thoroughly dissolved. Add orange juice and stir. Divide in half and pour
into two separate bowls. Pour the peaches and juice into
one half of the gelatin. Add lemon juice. Pour this mixture into a well greased mold and let set. Whip cream and
sugar. Add to gelatin in other bowl. Blend gently and pour
over first layer. Chill before serving.

Serves 8.

SUNSET MOLD

Brightens any table

    lemon gelatin--6 oz.
    boiling water--2 cups
    peeled apricots--1 lb. 14 oz. can
    sour cream--1/2 pint
    vanilla ice cream--1 cup, softened

Dissolve the gelatin in the water. Cool until almost set.
Drain and pit the apricots. Pour 1/2 cup of the gelatin in
the bottom of a 6 cup ring mold. Arrange 6 to 8 apricot
halves cut side up, in bottom of mold. Allow to set in refrigerator. Puree rest of apricots, using a blender if
available. Add to remaining gelatin. Whip sour cream and
softened ice cream together and fold into mixture. Pour
into mold and chill.

Serves 8.

RUBY MOLD

Very good served with brisket

    lemon gelatin--3 oz.
    hot water--3/4 cup
    fresh lemon juice--1 tablespoon
    shoestring beets--1 lb. can
    horseradish--1 teaspoon

Drain beets and reserve liquid. Dissolve lemon gelatin in
hot water. Combine lemon juice and beet liquid to make 1
cup (add water if necessary). Add juice to gelatin mixture.
Stir thoroughly. Add horseradish. Mix thoroughly. Chill
until syrupy. Add beets and pour into small mold.

Serves 5 to 6.

STRAWBERRY SURPRISE

Nice for a Chanukah buffet

    strawberry gelatin--12 oz.
    water--2 cups, boiling
    frozen strawberries--3 pkgs. (10 oz. each)
    crushed pineapple--13-1/2 oz. can
    fruit cocktail--17 oz. can
    bananas--3 medium, sliced
    chopped pecans--1 cup
    sour cream--1 pint

Dissolve gelatin in boiling water. Stir in strawberries,
pineapple, fruit cocktail, bananas, and pecans. Pour half
of the fruit mixture into a 3 quart jello mold and chill
until firm. Leave rest of mixture out at room temperature.
When gelatin in mold has become firm, spread sour cream over
it, and then carefully spoon remaining gelatin over sour
cream. Chill.

Serves 16.

****

"Upon thy summer fruits and upon thy vintage" (Jeremiah)

CHERRY MOLD

Gives red accent to a buffet table

    lemon gelatin--6 oz.
    boiling water--2 cups
    pitted black cherries--2 cans (11 oz. each)
    mandarin orange slices--11 oz. can
    brandy--1 oz.
    sliced almonds--2-1/2 oz.

Drain and reserve juices from cherries and mandarin orange slices. Dissolve gelatin in boiling water in a 4 cup measuring bowl. Add the fruit juices and brandy. Add ice cubes until the total liquid measures 3-1/2 cups. Stir until ice melts. Put into refrigerator until half set. Add fruit and nuts. Pour into a 6 cup lightly buttered mold. Serves 8.

AMBROSIA MOLD

The mold that has everything - beauty, flavor, raves

    lemon gelatin--9 oz.
    boiling water--4 cups
    unflavored gelatin--1 envelope (1 tablespoon)
    crushed pineapple--28 oz. (fruit and juice)
    cream cheese--6 oz.
    sour cream--8 oz.
    shredded coconut--1 cup, moist
    marshmallow miniatures--1 cup
    mandarin oranges--11 oz. can, drained

Dissolve lemon gelatin in the boiling water. Dissolve unflavored gelatin in juice from canned pineapple. Combine with lemon gelatin. Set in refrigerator until thick enough to whip.

Whip gelatin. Soften cream cheese with the sour cream. Mix cream cheese and sour cream mixture with coconut, marshmallows, and mandarin oranges. Fold into gelatin. Pour into 12 cup mold. Chill in refrigerator overnight or in freezer 1 hour. Remove by placing mold in hot water only 10 seconds. Go around edge with sharp knife. Place platter on top of mold. Invert plate and mold together.

Serves 40 women if the fund raising vice-president cuts, and 20 women if the program chairman serves the mold.

ROSY RHUBARB MOLD

Good, simple mold husbands like

    gelatin--strawberry (or favorite red), 15 oz.
    frozen sliced strawberries--10 oz. pkg., thawed
    crushed pineapple--20 oz. can, drained
    rhubarb--16 oz. can, drained and sliced
    water--6 cups

Dissolve gelatin in 6 cups hot water. When slightly thickened, add remaining ingredients. Pour into 12 cup mold and
chill. Serves 16.

RUSSIAN CREAM MOLD

Try the delicious cream layer with your favorite fruit mold

    unflavored gelatin--1 envelope (1 tablespoon)
    cold water--3 tablespoons
    sugar--1/2 cup
    cream--1/2 pint (8 oz.)
    water--almost 2 cups
    sour cream--1/2 pint (8 oz.)
    vanilla--1 teaspoon
    crushed pineapple--8 oz. can
    strawberry gelatin--6 oz.
    whole cranberries--16 oz. can
    chopped walnuts--1 cup

Sprinkle unflavored gelatin over 3 tablespoons of cold water.
Set aside. Bring sugar, cream, and 1 cup of water to a boil,
stirring constantly. Remove immediately from heat. Add
gelatin. Mix thoroughly until gelatin is dissolved. Blend
in sour cream. Add vanilla. Beat with rotary beater until
smooth. Pour into 2 quart greased mold and place in refrigerator until firm.

Meanwhile drain crushed pineapple. Measure juice and add
enough water to make 1 cup of liquid. Bring to a boil and
pour over strawberry gelatin. Stir well. Add the cranberries and nuts. Mix well. Cool. Prick the first layer of
jello in several places (to prevent second layer from slip-
ping). Pour over firm first layer. Chill.

Serves 16.

GREEN MOUNTAIN MOLD

One mashed avocado may be added if you so desire

crushed pineapple--16 oz. can
lime gelatin--12 oz.
hot water--24 oz. (3 cups)
sour cream--1 pint

Drain juice from can of crushed pineapple. Measure juice
and add enough cold water to make 2 cups of liquid. Reserve
pineapple and set aside liquid. Dissolve gelatin in hot
water and add pineapple juice. Stir thoroughly. Cool until
firm enough to whip. Beat in sour cream. Fold in crushed
pineapple. Pour into a well greased 3 quart mold. Chill
until firm.

Serves 16.

HELPFUL HINTS

Some are old,
Some are new.
We know there's one
that can help you!

Since all ovens are not uniform, check all baking at least fifteen
minutes before specified time on recipe. Then you judge how much
longer baking time should be allowed.

Always keep a small piece of clean wet sponge on top of wrapping paper
in brown sugar box after opening. Whenever you use the box, wet the
sponge. Your brown sugar will never cake.

Frost grapes by dipping in beaten egg white. Drain and turn in powdered sugar. The sugar may be tinted with food coloring.

Dip any fresh cut-up fruit in lemon juice to keep from discoloring.

When baking chicken, line pan with aluminum foil--it will be much
easier when washing time comes around.

Fish or onion odor can be removed from utensils and dishes by adding
1 teaspoon baking soda to dish water.

When using matzo meal in a recipe, always keep in mind that mixture
will thicken considerably if allowed to stand.

from borsht to bouillabaisse

TUNA BOMBAY

Best tuna salad yet

      tuna--2 cans (7 oz. each), flaked
      cooked rice (firm)--1-1/2 cups
      celery--1 cup, chopped
      mayonnaise--1/2 cup
      lemon juice--1 teaspoon
      curry powder--1/2 teaspoon
      pepper--1/8 teaspoon
      salt--1/8 teaspoon

      Condiments:

      salted peanuts--4 oz.
      mandarin oranges--11 oz. can
      raisins--3/4 cup
      fresh coconut chips--1 cup, toasted
      green onions--1/2 cup
      hard cooked eggs--2 large, riced

Flake tuna. Add rice, celery, mayonnaise, lemon juice, and
seasonings. Arrange on lettuce leaves and chill. In dishes
surrounding tuna, serve the condiments. Serves 8 to 10.

MARINATED VEGETABLE SALAD

Chapter Board enjoyed this salad

      green beans--2 cans (1 lb. each), tiny, whole
      petit pois (peas)--1 lb. can
      celery--small bunch, diced
      green pepper--1, diced
      pimiento--2 oz. jar, diced
      carrots--16 oz. can, diced
      oil--1/4 cup
      white vinegar--1 cup
      sugar--1/2 cup
      water--2 tablespoons
      salt--1/2 teaspoon
      pepper--1/8 teaspoon
      paprika--1/8 teaspoon

Drain vegetables well; put in salad bowl. Mix oil, vinegar,
sugar, water, and seasonings together. Pour over vegetables. Marinate 24 hours or less if you like a milder
flavor. Toss several times before serving. Drain.

BLEU CHEESE DRESSING

This can also be used as a dip for vegetables

      bleu cheese--1/4 lb., crumbled
      sour cream--1 cup
      lemon juice--3 tablespoons
      Worcestershire sauce--1 teaspoon
      garlic--one clove, crushed
      salt--1/4 teaspoon

Blend sour cream into cheese a little at a time, using a fork. Add other ingredients. Mix with a salad for eight.

WATERCRESS SALAD

A taste treat for you and your family

      watercress--3 bunches
      large fresh mushrooms--3/4 lb.
      oil--2/3 cup
      tarragon vinegar--1/4 cup
      garlic--1 clove, minced
      dry mustard--1/2 teaspoon
      salt--1 teaspoon
      sugar--1/2 teaspoon
      coarse ground pepper--1/2 teaspoon

Trim, wash, and dry watercress. Trim stems from mushrooms and wipe caps with a damp cloth. Slice mushroom caps thinly. Combine watercress and mushrooms in salad bowl. Combine remaining ingredients in screw-top jar or in blender. Shake or whirl to blend. Just before serving, toss salad lightly with dressing. Serves 8.

WHO MADE THE SALAD?

Always a great hit

mixed salad greens

parsley, chopped
cherry tomatoes or peeled wedges
olives--black and green
artichoke hearts--marinated or plain
radishes--sliced or cut as roses
pickled beets--shredded or sliced
green onions--sliced
red onion rings
cucumber slices
croutons
egg wedges
garbanzo beans
carrots--sliced or shredded
celery--slivered
zucchini--thinly sliced
capers
asparagus
tuna fish
anchovies

cheese cubes (for dairy dinners)

slivered chicken, beef and salami (for meat dinners)

Italian salad dressing
bleu cheese dressing
French dressing

Place salad greens in large serving bowl. Put a selection
of the accompaniments in separate bowls. Pour salad dress-
ings into gravy boats. Let each guest help himself to the
salad, mixing any combination he wishes.

DIETER'S SALAD DRESSING

High protein--low fat

ranch salad dressing--1 envelope
buttermilk--2 cups
low-fat cottage cheese--1 pint
dry onions--1 oz.

Blend salad dressing mix, buttermilk, and cottage cheese in blender. Mix in onions and keep in refrigerator overnight. Very good on slaw.

CAESAR SALAD

A famous favorite

    garlic--2 medium cloves, crushed
    olive oil--6 tablespoons
    wine vinegar--2 tablespoons
    fresh lemon juice--1 tablespoon
    Worcestershire sauce--1/2 teaspoon
    dry mustard--1 teaspoon
    salt--1/2 teaspoon
    fresh ground pepper--1 teaspoon
    Parmesan cheese--2-1/2 tablespoons
    anchovies--1 can
    egg--1, coddled (boil 1-1/2 minutes)
    lettuce--1 head, broken into bite size pieces
    garlic croutons--1/2 cup

Put garlic, olive oil, vinegar, and lemon juice in a large salad bowl. Mix well. Add Worcestershire sauce, mustard, salt, pepper, cheese, anchovies (cut in small pieces with some of the oil), and coddled egg and blend well. Add lettuce and toss until well blended. Drop croutons on top of salad. Serve immediately.

Serves 6.

GREEN GODDESS DRESSING

The Hadassah women liked what they tasted

    mayonnaise--1 cup
    salt--1/4 to 1/2 teaspoon
    dry mustard--1/2 teaspoon
    anchovy paste--2 teaspoons
    Worcestershire sauce--1 teaspoon
    garlic--1 clove, grated or crushed
    chives (or green onions)--2 to 3 tablespoons, chopped
    egg--1 large, hard cooked, grated

Using electric mixer, combine all ingredients well. Best
used the first day.

PETITE PEA SALAD

Nice with barbecue or for a summer party

    petite peas--4 pkgs., frozen (10 oz. each)
    Spanish onion--1/2 cup, sliced thin
    mayonnaise--1/2 cup
    prepared mustard--1 tablespoon
    seasoned salt--1/2 teaspoon
    seasoned pepper--1/8 teaspoon
    egg--1 large, cooked, grated
    romaine lettuce--garnish

Cook peas for one minute. Drain well. Mix with onion,
mayonnaise, mustard, salt, and pepper. Marinate 3 to 4
hours or overnight. Put in bowl lined with romaine lettuce
and sprinkle with grated egg just before serving. Serves 18.

RYE SLAW

This is a nice change from regular slaw

        caraway seeds--1/4 cup
        oil--1 cup
        white vinegar--1/4 cup
        sugar--1 tablespoon
        salt--1/4 teaspoon
        pepper--1/8 teaspoon
        cabbage--1 large

Shred cabbage fine. Mix other ingredients and pour over
cabbage. Refrigerate for several hours before serving.

FRESH SPINACH SALAD

Beats taking iron pills

    spinach--1 lb.
    garlic--1 clove, crushed
    oil--4 tablespoons
    red wine vinegar--2 tablespoons
    tarragon--1/16 teaspoon
    salt--1/2 teaspoon
    pepper--1/8 teaspoon
    sugar--1 tablespoon
    egg--1 large, slightly beaten
    green onions--6, chopped coarsely
    egg--1 large, hard cooked, chopped
    beef fry--3 slices, fried crisp and crumbled

Wash spinach to be sure all sand is out. Cut off roots and
discard wilted leaves. Cut into bite size pieces. Add
crushed garlic to 1 tablespoon of oil. Trickle over salad.
Mix 3 tablespoons of oil, vinegar, spices, salt, sugar, and
slightly beaten egg in a small saucepan. Heat until liquid
starts to thicken or changes color. Pour hot dressing over
salad. Garnish with egg, onions, and beef fry.

Serve immediately. Serves 4.

ONE HUNDRED FULL MOONS

Something for the family to nibble on

    salt--1/2 teaspoon
    sugar--1 teaspoon
    cider vinegar--2 tablespoons
    sour cream--1/2 pint (1 cup)
    green onions or chives--2 tablespoons, chopped
    dried dill weed--1/2 teaspoon
    celery seed--1 teaspoon
    cucumbers--2, about 8" long

Dissolve salt and sugar in vinegar. Add sour cream, a
little at a time, blending well. Add green onions, dill,
and celery seed.

Peel cucumbers. Slice in 1/8" rounds. Cover with sauce.
Mix well and chill one hour before serving. Serves 4.

CURRY SALAD

A delightful main dish for a summer luncheon

        tuna--15 oz.
        eggs--4 large, hard cooked
        green onions--1/4 cup
        celery--1 cup
        green pepper--1/2 cup, chopped
        curry--1 tablespoon
        salt--1/2 teaspoon
        pepper--1/8 teaspoon
        lemon juice--3 tablespoons
        mayonnaise--1 cup
        pineapple chunks--8 oz. can
        lettuce--2 large heads

Drain and flake tuna. Chop eggs, onions, celery, and mix
together. Add the rest of the ingredients, except lettuce.
Refrigerate until ready to serve. Wash lettuce and tear in
bite size pieces. Pour tuna mixture over lettuce and toss.
Serve immediately. Serves 8.

CHINESE CHICKEN SALAD

Just like you get in Chinatown

chicken breasts--2, cooked
cooking oil--2 cups
bean curd noodles--1/4 lb. (buy in Japanese market)
celery--5 stalks, sliced
fresh mushrooms--1/4 lb., sliced
green onions--5, sliced
carrot--1, grated coarsely
iceberg lettuce--2 heads, cold and crisp
almonds--4 tablespoons, sliced and toasted

Dressing:

wine vinegar--2 tablespoons
oil--4 tablespoons
white vinegar--2 tablespoons
sugar--1 teaspoon
pepper--1/4 teaspoon
monosodium glutamate--1/4 teaspoon
Chinese sesame oil--1 tablespoon
soy sauce--2 tablespoons
salt--1/2 teaspoon

Slice chicken. Set aside. Heat 2 cups of cooking oil. Put in a strand of noodle. If it swells and rises to the top, add the rest. Noodles are done as soon as they swell. Drain noodles. Set aside. Mix together celery, mushrooms, onions, carrots and almonds. Break lettuce into bite size pieces and place in large bowl. Cover with vegetable mixture. Arrange chicken and noodles on top.

Mix ingredients for a dressing. Pour over salad just before serving. Serves 6. Try substituting 2 cups of bean sprouts for the lettuce and you'll have my husband's favorite salad.

AMBROSIA SALAD

mandarin oranges--1 cup, drained
pineapple tid-bits--1 cup, drained
coconut--1 cup
marshmallows--1 cup, miniature
sour cream--1/2 pint (1 cup)

Mix ingredients together. Keep in refrigerator 24 hours before serving. Serves 8 to 10.

UNUSUAL POTATO SALAD

A change of pace

        potatoes--3 lbs., cooked in jackets
        frozen peas and carrots--10 oz. pkg.
        garbanzo beans--16 oz. can, well drained
        eggs--6 large, hard cooked, grated
        sour cream--3/4 cup
        mayonnaise--3/4 cup
        onion soup mix--1-1/2 oz. envelope
        curry-1/8 teaspoon
        mustard--1 teaspoon
        salt--1 teaspoon
        sugar--1 teaspoon
        monosodium glutamate--1/4 teaspoon
        paprika--1/4 teaspoon

Cook peas and carrots slightly. Peel and cut potatoes into
squares, add carrots, peas, garbanzo beans, and eggs. In a
separate bowl mix sour cream, mayonnaise, and onion soup
mix; add seasonings and pour over potatoes. Mix well.
Sprinkle with paprika. This may be prepared a day in
advance of serving. Serves 12.

CARROT SALAD

Good source of vitamin C, vitamin A, and iron

raisins--1/2 cup, dark
pineapple juice--1/2 cup
carrots--2 cups, grated
pineapple tid-bits--1/2 cup
nuts--1/4 cup (walnuts or pecans), chopped
mayonnaise--2 tablespoons

Soak raisins in pineapple juice overnight. Next day, grate
carrots. Mix with raisins in pineapple juice. Add all
other ingredients and mix well. Serves 6.

VIENNA POTATO SALAD

A complement for a cold buffet

    potatoes--2-1/2 lbs.
    vinegar--1/4 cup
    water--1/4 cup
    liquid from dill pickles--1/4 cup
    onions--1/4 cup, chopped
    celery--1/4 cup, chopped
    dill pickle--1/4 cup, chopped
    salt--1 teaspoon
    pepper--1/2 teaspoon
    oil--1/2 cup
    beef fry--2 slices, fried crisp and crumbled

Boil potatoes until done, but not soft. Peel and dice into
bowl. Boil vinegar, water, and pickle marinade for a minute
and pour over potatoes. Let set for 20 minutes. Add onions,
celery, pickles, salt and pepper, and beef fry. Pour oil
over top. Mix well.

This salad may be served hot, if preferred. Serves 5.

TUNA LIME SALAD

Serve for lunch with cheese and fruit

    slivered almonds--1/4 cup plus 1 tablespoon, toasted
    tuna--26 oz. (approximately), flaked
    canned seedless grapes--1 cup, drained
    salt--3/4 teaspoon
    white pepper--1/4 teaspoon
    mayonnaise--3/4 cup
    nutmeg--1/2 teaspoon
    lime rind--1 teaspoon, grated
    lime juice--2 tablespoons
    pineapple tid-bits--1 lb. can, drained

Set aside 1 tablespoon of almonds. Combine all other ingredients. Place in a serving bowl lined with romaine lettuce.
Cover with almonds. Refrigerate.

Serves 16.

GAZPACHO SOUP

My kids say, "Mmmmmmmm, good."

fresh ground pepper--1/8 teaspoon
beef bouillon--2 cups, canned
tomatoes--4 medium, diced
green pepper--1-1/2 cups, chopped
onion--3/4 cup, chopped
garlic--1 clove, minced
lemon juice--1/2 cup (2 lemons)
olive oil--1/4 cup
paprika--1 tablespoon
salt--1 teaspoon

eggs--2 large, hard cooked, riced
green onions--1 cup, chopped
cucumber--1 cup, diced

Combine all ingredients except for eggs, green onions, and cucumbers. Let stand at room temperature for 1 hour, stirring frequently. Chill at least 2 hours. Serve in tureen and pass the eggs, green onions, and diced cucumber separately. Serves 6.

INSTANT CHICKEN SOUP

Use with matzo balls

dried chicken noodle soup with diced chicken--1 envelope
chicken broth--2 cans
water

Prepare soup mix according to directions. Add chicken broth plus 2 cups of water. Prepare matzo balls in the morning while soup is cooking. Allow matzo balls to permeate the soup during the day. It tastes like home-made, so sit back and wait for the compliments.

Soup with matzo balls may also be frozen.

Serves 8.

****

"The black cummin is beaten out with a staff" (Isaiah)

48

CABBAGE BORSHT

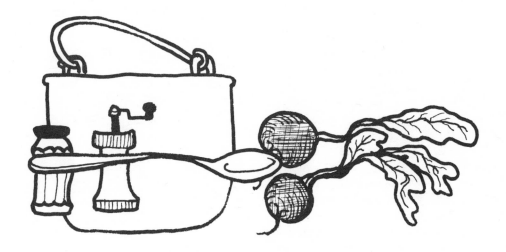

A modern twist for an old fashioned recipe

    flanken--2 lbs.
    marrow bones--1 lb.
    cabbage--2 lbs., white, shredded
    onion--1 large, diced
    apples--2 large, pippin, peeled and diced
    tomato sauce--2 cans (8 oz. each)
    barbecue sauce--1/4 cup
    salt--2 to 3 teaspoons
    water--2 quarts
    shredded beets--16 oz. can, undrained
    fresh lemon juice--1 tablespoon
    sugar--1/4 teaspoon

Place meat and bones in large soup pot. Add cabbage, onion,
apples, tomato sauce, barbecue sauce, 2 teaspoons salt, and
water. Bring to a boil and simmer covered 1-1/2 hours or
until meat is tender. Add beets, lemon juice, and sugar and
more salt, if needed. Remove from heat. Remove meat, cut
into small pieces, and return to soup. Cook 15 minutes more.

HOME-MADE CHICKEN SOUP

Like my mother used to make

        chicken--pullet, 6 lbs., cut in pieces
        chicken giblets
        salt--1-1/2 teaspoons
        water--to cover
        onion--1 large
        carrots--2 large, peeled
        parsnip--1 medium, peeled
        celery--3 stalks, including leaves
        parsley--1/2 bunch, tied with white thread

Place chicken pieces in large soup pot. Add water to cover
chicken, but no more. Add salt. Bring to a boil. Skim
off top. Add onion, carrots, parsnip, and celery. Cover.
Cook until chicken is tender, adding parsley 15 minutes before soup is done. Taste and add salt if needed. Remove
chicken and serve separately. Add noodles, rice, or kasha
to soup before serving.

Like another mother used to make

Follow instructions as above omitting parsnip, but doubling
amount of carrots and celery used. One fresh tomato and
1/8 teaspoon pepper may be added. Strain when done. This
is the traditional chicken soup used when serving matzo
balls and kreplach.

Serves 8.

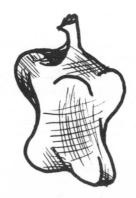

*"Set on the pot, set it on, and also pour water into it:
Gather into it the pieces belonging to it, even every good
piece, the thigh, and the shoulder; fill it with the choice
bones....Make it boil well." (Ezekiel)*

MATZO BALLS SUPREME

Light and fluffy every time

eggs--6 large, separated
chicken fat--1 tablespoon
white pepper--1/4 teaspoon
salt--1 teaspoon
nutmeg--just a dash
matzo meal--1-1/4 cups

Beat egg yolks, add melted chicken fat, and seasonings.
Beat egg whites well and fold in the yolks. Gradually fold
in the matzo meal. This will be a soft mixture. Allow mixture to stand up to 2 hours to thicken but no longer. Dip
hands in water to prevent sticking. Make walnut sized
balls.

Into large kettle of boiling, salted water gently place
each ball, cover pan, and boil for 1/2 hour. Serve with
chicken soup - naturally!

Yield: 14 to 16

KREPLACH

The trick is not to use water!!!

flour--1 cup plus 2 tablespoons
salt--1 teaspoon
eggs--2 large, slightly beaten
ground beef--1/4 lb.
onion--2 tablespoons, chopped
seasoning salt--1/8 teaspoon
chicken soup or bouillon--3 quarts

Gradually mix salt and flour into eggs. Knead until smooth.
Roll out into a thin sheet 14" x 18". Use plenty of flour
to prevent sticking. Cut into 2" squares.

Mix meat with onion and seasoning salt. Put less than a
teaspoon of meat in the center of each square. Fold over
one point making a triangular wedge. Press edges firmly
together. Drop into 3 quarts of boiling soup. Cover.
Simmer 1/2 hour.

LIMA BEAN BARLEY SOUP

A good hearty soup

        soup meat--1-1/2 lbs.
        soup bones--1-1/2 lbs.
        water--3 quarts
        onion--1, chopped
        salt--2 teaspoons
        pepper--1/16 teaspoon
        pearl barley--1 cup
        parsnip--1, chopped
        carrots--4, chopped
        celery--4 stalks, chopped
        frozen lima beans--10 oz. pkg., thawed
        parsley flakes--1 tablespoon

In a deep pot combine beef bones, beef and water. Bring to
a boil, and skim. Add onion, salt, and pepper. Cover. Simmer 1 hour. Add barley, parsnip, carrots, and celery and
simmer 1 more hour. Add lima beans and taste to see if more
salt or pepper is needed. Also add more water a little at a
time if you think soup is too thick, and cook until meat
and vegetables are tender. Add parsley after soup has
cooked 50 minutes. Serves 12.

FAKE BEET BORSHT

        shredded beets--16 oz. can, undrained
        water--2 cups
        frozen lemonade--2 oz., thawed
        sugar--1/2 teaspoon
        salt--3/4 teaspoon
        sour cream--1/2 cup

Mix together beets, sugar, and salt. Add water and gradually add lemonade. Chill. Garnish with a scoop of sour cream.
Serves 6.

QUICK BEET BORSHT

        shredded beets--16 oz. can
        water--2 cups
        lemon juice--2 tablespoons
        sugar--2 teaspoons
        salt--3/4 teaspoon
        egg--1 large
        sour cream--1/2 cup

Drain beets. In blender add beet juice, water, lemon juice,
sugar, salt, egg, and sour cream. Blend thoroughly. Add
beets and blend 30 seconds. Chill.

MACHIAH MATZO BALLS

You can even open the window and these won't fail

            eggs-4 large
            schmaltz (chicken fat)--1/4 cup
            matzo meal--3/4 cup
            salt--1/2 teaspoon
            baking powder--1/4 teaspoon

Beat eggs slightly. Add fat and dry ingredients. Set in refrigerator for 4 hours. Shape into 1" balls. Drop into boiling canned soup, bouillon, or salted water (3 quarts). Cover and boil for 25 minutes. Transfer them to your good home-made soup when ready to serve.

Makes 20 matzo balls.

HELPFUL HINTS

To keep that freshly baked texture, when defrosting frozen cakes, remove wrapping immediately.

The first step in preparing your favorite chicken recipe, to enhance the flavor, dip chicken in mixture of half lemon juice and half cold water.

from tzimmes to spinach

FRENCH VEGETABLES

A good way to conserve your vitamins

Plunge vegetable into a large kettle of rapidly boiling salted water. As soon as they are barely tender, drain and cover with cold water (to stop cooking and set color). Drain again immediately. Just before serving, toss them briefly in hot butter and seasonings.

This is a fine method of cooking green beans, peas, broccoli, cauliflower, asparagus, carrots, or squash.

56

SWISS CASSEROLE

No wonder the Swiss are famous for their food

    frozen French cut green beans--4 pkgs. (10 oz. each)
    butter--2 tablespoons
    flour--2 tablespoons
    sour cream--1/2 pint (1 cup)
    sugar--1 teaspoon
    salt--1 teaspoon
    onion--1 tablespoon, grated
    Swiss cheese--1/2 lb., grated
    cornflake crumbs--1/2 cup
    butter--2 teaspoons, melted

Cook green beans according to directions on package until
almost tender, drain, and set aside. Melt 2 tablespoons butter, add flour, and cook until smooth. Remove from heat and
add sour cream, sugar, salt, and onion. Mix thoroughly; return to stove and cook until thickened. Combine sauce and
beans. Place in a buttered casserole. Sprinkle Swiss cheese
over top. Combine cornflake crumbs with melted butter and
sprinkle over cheese. Bake uncovered at 400°F for 35 minutes. (Your family won't resist vegetables with a recipe
like this one.) Serves 12.

ALMOND CAULIFLOWER

I could eat this with every meal

        cauliflower--1-1/2 lbs.
        salt--1 teaspoon
        slivered almonds--1/2 cup
        butter--4 tablespoons
        garlic--1 clove, minced
        soft bread crumbs--1 cup

Cut or break cauliflower into separate flowers. Cover with
boiling water and boil uncovered 10 minutes. Remove from
heat. Add salt. Cover and allow to cook off heat about 5
more minutes. Meanwhile, saute almonds in butter, add
garlic and bread crumbs, and saute until lightly browned.
Drain cauliflower and cover with nut mixture. Serve hot.

If frozen cauliflower is preferred, use 20 oz. Serves 8.

BROCCOLI MOLD

This is definitely party fare

```
frozen chopped broccoli--10 oz., thawed
parsley--2 sprigs
green onions--1/8 cup, chopped
water--2 tablespoons
butter--1-1/2 tablespoons
flour--1-1/2 tablespoons
sour cream--1/2 cup
cheddar or Swiss cheese--1/4 cup, grated
eggs--2 large, well beaten
pepper--1/8 teaspoon
nutmeg--1/4 teaspoon
salt--1/2 teaspoon
```

Place broccoli, parsley, onions, and water in blender and chop. Melt butter, stir in flour, sour cream, and cheese. Add to broccoli mixture. Cook until cheese melts. Take off heat. Stir in eggs. Add spices and salt. Put into a well greased casserole. Bake at 350°F for 1 hour.

You may double the recipe and bake in an 8 cup ring mold. Slivered almonds or crushed cornflakes may garnish top.

Serves 4.

CARROT TZIMMES

Like Daddy used to make

```
brisket--3 lbs.
salt--2 teaspoons
pepper--1/8 teaspoon
onions--2 large, chopped
water--2 cups
carrots--2 bunches, sliced
ginger--1 teaspoon
corn syrup--1 cup
brown sugar--1 cup
potatoes--2 large, grated
flour--1/2 cup
eggs--2 large
chicken fat--2 tablespoons, rendered
onions--1/2 cup, chopped and sauteed
```

Rub meat with 1 teaspoon salt and pepper. Place in Dutch oven fat side down. Bake at 450°F 30 minutes uncovered. Turn several times. Add uncooked onions. Cook 15 minutes uncovered or until onions brown. Pour off melted fat. Reduce oven to 350°F. Add water, carrots, 1/2 teaspoon ginger, corn syrup, and brown sugar. Bake covered for 90 minutes.

Mix potatoes, flour, eggs, 1 teaspoon salt, 1/2 teaspoon ginger, chicken fat, and sauteed onions. Spoon over carrots. Cover and continue to cook at 350°F for 1 hour. Serves 5.

Add 1/4 lb. prunes last hour of baking, if desired, for the old world flavor.

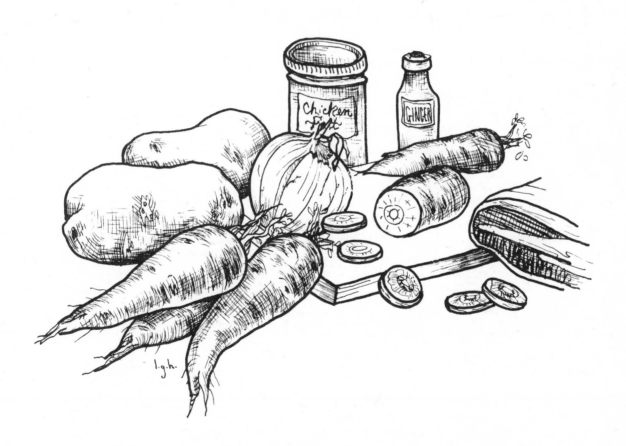

CARROTS AND COGNAC

My non-carrot eaters love these carrots

        frozen sliced carrots--1-1/2 lbs.
        butter--1/2 cup (do not substitute)
        sugar--1-1/2 teaspoons
        salt--1 teaspoon
        cognac--1/2 cup

Melt butter in bottom of 2 quart casserole. Stir in sugar,
salt, and carrots. Cover and bake at 350°F for 45 minutes.
Add cognac. Keep covered until served.

This is especially nice served with a fish plate and salad
as carrots add color. This party fare freezes well.

GREEN BEANS

Food for company

        onion--1 medium, minced
        butter--3 tablespoons
        green beans--3-1/2 cups, cooked
        tomato sauce--3/4 cup
        salt--1/2 teaspoon
        sugar--1/2 teaspoon
        lemon juice--2 teaspoons
        pepper--1/8 teaspoon

Cook onion in butter until tender, 3 to 4 minutes. Add rest
of ingredients. Heat thoroughly, stirring occasionally.
If you use canned green beans, you may want to cut the salt
slightly. Serves 8.

BROCCOLI AND ONIONS

Remember that broccoli is a very high source of Vitamin C

    frozen broccoli spears--2 pkgs. (10 oz. each), thawed
    cheddar cheese--1 cup, shredded
    French fried onions--3-1/2 oz. can
    cream of mushroom soup--10-1/2 oz. can
    milk--1/3 cup
    French dressing mix--2-1/2 teaspoons

60

Place broccoli in bottom of 2 quart casserole. Mix cheese,
soup, milk, French dressing mix, and 2/3 of onions. Pour
over broccoli. Bake at 325°F for 20 minutes. Sprinkle remaining onions on top. Bake 3 more minutes. Serves 6.

DREAM CASSEROLE

A wonderful party dish

    frozen green beans--2 pkgs. (10 oz. each)
    bean sprouts--16 oz. can, drained
    water chestnuts--8 oz. can, drained
    sliced mushrooms--4 oz. can, drained
    cream of mushroom soup--2 cans (10-1/2 oz. each)
    French fried onion rings--1 can

Arrange thawed and drained green beans in bottom of 8" x
13" glass baking dish. Layer bean sprouts, water chestnuts,
and mushrooms over beans. Cover with soup. Bake uncovered
at 350°F for 30 minutes. Sprinkle onions over top and continue baking for 10 more minutes.

Serves 10.

BRUSSELS SPROUTS

Sprouts with a spark

    brussels sprouts--1 lb., fresh or frozen
    salt--1/2 teaspoon
    pepper--1/8 teaspoon
    butter--4 tablespoons
    lemon juice--3 tablespoons
    lemon rind--1/2 teaspoon, grated
    parsley--1/3 cup, finely chopped
    egg whites--2 large, hard cooked, finely chopped

Drop brussels sprouts into 1 quart of briskly boiling water.
Boil uncovered until sprouts are firm but tender when tested with a fork. Drain immediately. Place in heated serving dish. Add salt and pepper.

Brown butter to a golden color. Pour over sprouts.
Sprinkle with lemon juice and rind, egg, and parsley.

Serves 4.

ISRAELI PANCAKES

Not a griddle cake!

```
frozen chopped spinach--10 oz. pkg., thawed
salt--1-3/4 teaspoons
pepper--1/8 teaspoon
garlic powder--1/4 teaspoon
fresh mushrooms--1/4 lb., chopped
eggs--2 large, separated
baking powder--1/2 teaspoon
flour--1 tablespoon
dried onions--1 tablespoon
oil--3 tablespoons
```

Drain uncooked spinach thoroughly in colander. Press out all water with the back of a large spoon. Combine drained spinach, salt, pepper, garlic powder, mushrooms, egg yolks, baking powder, flour, and onions. Mix thoroughly.

In separate bowl, beat egg whites until stiff, but not dry. Fold into above mixture. Heat oil in heavy skillet. Spoon 1 tablespoon batter at a time into oil to make pancakes. Cook on both sides until golden brown.

Remove and drain on absorbent paper. To keep warm, place on cookie sheet covered with aluminum foil. Place in 250°F oven until ready to serve. Makes a dozen 3" cakes.

ARTICHOKE CASSEROLE

This makes a nice dish to serve with a chicken entree

```
marinated artichoke hearts--6 oz. drained
frozen chopped spinach--10 oz. pkg., thawed and drained
sour cream--1/2 pint (1 cup)
Parmesan cheese--1/2 cup, grated
```

Place artichokes in greased 1 quart baking dish. Cover with the drained spinach. Mix sour cream to soften and spread over spinach carefully. Cover with grated cheese. Bake at 350°F for about 20 minutes or just until topping sets, or spinach will be over-cooked. Re-heats well.

Serves 6.

GLAZED BROCCOLI

Make now - bake later

        frozen broccoli--2 pkgs. (10 oz. each), thawed
        salt--1/2 teaspoon
        margarine--4 tablespoons
        flour--4 tablespoons
        non-dairy cream--1 cup
        bouillon soup--3/4 cup
        dry sherry--2 tablespoons
        lemon juice--2 tablespoons
        pepper--1/16 teaspoon
        monosodium glutamate--1/16 teaspoon
        slivered almonds--1/4 cup, blanched

Cook broccoli in boiling salted water no more than 5 minutes. Arrange in bottom of shallow 8" x 12" baking dish.

Melt margarine and quickly stir in flour. Remove from heat
and stir in non-dairy cream a little at a time. Add bouillon and cook over slow heat until thickened. Add sherry,
lemon juice, and seasonings. Pour over broccoli. Sprinkle
top with nuts. Bake at 375°F for 20 minutes. Serves 6.

GOURMET SPINACH

Elegant - good for dinner party

        fresh spinach--1 lb. or frozen chopped--10 oz. pkg.
        salt--1/2 teaspoon
        whipped cottage cheese--1 cup
        eggs--2 large, beaten
        caraway seed--1 teaspoon
        seasoned salt--1 teaspoon
        seasoned pepper--1/4 teaspoon
        nutmeg--1/8 teaspoon
        sharp cheddar cheese--1/2 cup, grated
        chopped almonds--2 tablespoons
        paprika--1/2 teaspoon

Wash fresh spinach, removing coarse stems. Cook in small
amount of salted boiling water until barely tender. Drain
well and chop fine, or cook frozen chopped spinach as directed on label and drain. Add salt, cottage cheese, eggs,
and seasonings. Put in greased 8" pie pan and sprinkle
with cheddar cheese and nuts. Bake at 350°F about 25 minutes; then sprinkle with paprika. Serves 4.

SPINACH CASSEROLE

Good for big family dinners

    frozen chopped spinach--4 pkgs. (10 oz. each)
    sour cream--1 pint (2 cups)
    onion soup mix--1 envelope (1-1/2 oz.)

Cook spinach as directed on package but omit salt. Drain
and press out water. Mix spinach with sour cream and onion
soup mix. Put in 3 quart round casserole and bake at 350°F
for 30 minutes.

Serves 12.

FRENCH SPINACH

A delicious creamed spinach

    butter--3 tablespoons
    flour--3 tablespoons
    half and half, or milk--1/2 cup
    onions--1/4 cup, grated
    garlic--1 clove, crushed
    salt--1/2 teaspoon
    pepper--1/8 teaspoon
    frozen chopped spinach--10 oz. pkg., cooked and drained

Melt butter in 1 quart saucepan. Blend in flour. Continue
to cook for another minute. Stir to prevent burning. Remove from heat. Blend in cream. Add onions and cook until
thick. Add garlic and seasonings. Add spinach and re-heat.

Serves 3.

NUTTY POPEYE CASSEROLE

    frozen chopped spinach--2 pkgs. (10 oz. each)
    cream of mushroom soup--10-1/2 oz. can
    cheddar cheese--1/2 cup, shredded
    chopped walnuts--1/2 cup

Cook spinach according to directions on the package. Drain
in colander. Place in bowl and mix with other ingredients.
Pour into a 2 quart casserole. Bake at 350°F for 30
minutes.

Serves 8.

SUMMER SQUASH
Nice vegetable for company

    summer squash--1-1/2 lbs.
    water--1 quart
    salt--1 teaspoon
    processed American cheese spread--8 oz.
    rich, flaky crackers--14, crumbled

    Topping:

    cheddar cheese-1/4 cup, shredded
    rich, flaky crackers--4, crumbled
    butter--1 tablespoon

Remove stems and wash summer squash thoroughly. Cut in
wedges. Place squash in salted water. Bring to a boil.
Simmer 10 minutes. Drain thoroughly. Mix squash, cheese,
and crackers and place in a greased glass baking dish.
Sprinkle with cheddar cheese and rest of crackers and dot
with butter. Bake at 350°F for 20 minutes until hot and
bubbly and golden brown.

APPLES AND SQUASH

A dieter's delight

    apples--6 peeled and cored (Rome Beauty)
    lemon juice--1/4 cup
    brown sugar substitute--1/2 cup
    cinnamon--1 teaspoon
    nutmeg--1/2 teaspoon
    frozen banana squash--7 oz., cooked and drained
    lemon diet drink--3/4 cup
    fresh mint, orange peel flowers, and cloves for
      decoration

Dip apples in lemon juice to keep from turning brown. Roll
each apple in brown sugar substitute. Place in baking dish.
Add cinnamon and nutmeg to squash. Fill core of each apple
with squash. Pour small amount of diet drink in bottom of
baking dish. Occasionally baste apples, adding more lemon
drink as you baste. Bake at 325°F for 1-1/2 hours.

Serve on platter decorated with fresh mint and orange peel
flowers. (Cut a flower out of a piece of orange peel. Put
a clove in center of the flower.)

65

CORN PIE

Excellent for barbecues

     whole chili peppers--3 oz. can
     creamed corn--16 oz. can
     corn meal--1/2 cup
     sugar--2 tablespoons
     milk--1/2 cup
     butter--3 tablespoons
     cheddar cheese--1 cup, grated

Cut chili in strips, removing heavy vein and seeds. Add corn, corn meal, sugar, milk, half of cheese, and butter. Pour into well greased 9" glass pie plate. Will be thin and runny. Sprinkle remaining cheese on top.

Bake at 400°F for 30 minutes.

Serves 6.

STUFFED ZUCCHINI

This is a welcome addition to any plate

    frozen chopped spinach--10 oz. package
    zucchini--3 large
    milk--1/2 cup
    salt--1/2 teaspoon
    cheddar cheese--3/4 cup, shredded, firmly packed
    butter--1 tablespoon
    bread crumbs--1/2 cup
    Parmesan cheese--1/4 cup

Cook spinach according to directions and drain well. Cut
off blossom end of zucchini and cook in small amount of
water, 10 to 12 minutes. Cool, cut into halves lengthwise
and scoop out pulp. Chop pulp and combine with cooked
spinach. Place zucchini shells in a greased shallow baking
dish. In saucepan, heat milk and add salt and cheddar
cheese. Cook and stir until sauce is smooth (about 5 minutes). Combine cheese sauce with vegetables and spoon into
zucchini shells. Melt butter and combine with bread crumbs
and Parmesan cheese and sprinkle over zucchini. Bake at
350°F for 20 minutes.

Serves 6.

GREEN PEAS

Italian style

oil--1/4 cup
onions--1-1/2 cups (thinly sliced)
fresh tomatoes--2 cups, diced
salt--1-1/2 teaspoons
pepper--1/2 teaspoon
oregano--1/4 teaspoon
frozen peas--2 pkgs. (10 oz. each), thawed

Heat oil in saucepan and saute onions 5 minutes. Mix in
all other ingredients. Cover and cook over low heat for
15 minutes.

Serves 6.

SPICED EGGPLANT

A really different combination

potato--1 large, peeled and diced
water--3/4 cup
oil--5 tablespoons
eggplant--2 cups, peeled and diced
onions--2 tablespoons, chopped
salt--3/4 teaspoon
dry mustard--3/4 teaspoon
turmeric--3/4 teaspoon
ginger--1/8 teaspoon
cayenne pepper--1/8 teaspoon
paprika--1/2 teaspoon

Bring potatoes to a boil in water. Boil for 2 minutes.
Drain potatoes, saving liquid. Heat oil in 10" heavy skillet. Add cooked potatoes. Add the rest of ingredients except for paprika. Cook until vegetables have browned, stirring frequently. Add liquid from potatoes. Cover. Cook
until water has evaporated and vegetables are tender (10 to
15 minutes). Add paprika for color and serve immediately.

Makes 4 to 6 servings.

ACORN SQUASH

acorn squash--2 medium
onion--2 tablespoons, chopped
butter--4 tablespoons
cheddar cheese--1 cup, grated
salt--1 teaspoon
pepper--1/4 teaspoon
creamed corn--8 oz. can

Bake squash at 400°F for 30 to 40 minutes or until tender.
Cut into quarters. Discard seeds and scoop out center,
leaving about a 1/4" thick shell. Mash pulp and mix with
other ingredients. Fill shells with pulp. Bake at 350°F
for 15 minutes. Slip under broiler a few minutes to brown
tops.

Serves 4.

RATATOUILLE

An authentic French vegetable stew without meat

eggplant--2 medium (about 2 lbs. total), unpeeled and diced
zucchini--4 medium (about 6" each), unpeeled and diced
water--1 cup
onions--2 large, chopped coarsely
green pepper--1 medium, diced
olive oil--2 tablespoons
pepper--1/16 tablespoon
salt--1/2 teaspoon
sweet basil--1/2 teaspoon
coriander seed--1 teaspoon
garlic--1 clove, crushed
tomatoes--3, chopped

Put eggplant and zucchini in 4 quart Dutch oven. Add water.
Simmer uncovered until water disappears. Add onions, green
pepper, and oil. Continue to fry with eggplant and zucchini
for 3 minutes. Add seasonings. Bake at 350°F for 40 minutes. Add tomatoes and cook another 25 minutes.

May be re-warmed but it is good even cold. Serves 10.

CINDERELLA'S SLIPPERS

Can be served at any ball

```
zucchini--6 medium
eggs--2 large, well beaten
cheddar cheese--4 oz., grated
jack cheese--1/2 cup, grated
bread crumbs--1/2 cup
parsley--2 tablespoons, chopped
salt--1/2 teaspoon
pepper--1/8 teaspoon
Parmesan cheese--1 tablespoon
```

Cut off ends of zucchini and scrub. Boil zucchini in water until cooked, but still very firm. Cut in halves, lengthwise. Scoop out center pulp with spoon and invert slipper to drain. Mix remaining ingredients, except for Parmesan cheese, with pulp and fill slippers. Arrange in greased baking dish. Sprinkle with Parmesan cheese. Bake in uncovered dish 350°F for 15 minutes. Turn oven up to 450°F for 5 minutes or until top is brown.

Do not freeze.

Serves 12.

EGGPLANT PARMESAN

A delicious non-meat treat

Sauce:

olive oil--2 tablespoons
onions--1-1/2 cups, chopped
stewed tomatoes--2 cups
basil--1 teaspoon
salt--1/2 teaspoon
pepper--1/8 teaspoon

eggplant--6 slices, fried
Mozzarella cheese--1 lb.
Parmesan cheese--3 oz., grated

Fry onions in olive oil until transparent. Add tomatoes and spices. Simmer for about 10 minutes.

Arrange eggplant in "oven to table" 12" x 12" container. Cover with the sauce. Slice Mozzarella cheese into 6" thick slices and place 1 slice over each piece of eggplant. Cover with the Parmesan cheese.

Bake at 400°F for 20 minutes, covered. Uncover, bake 10 minutes more. Do not over cook or cheese becomes rubbery.

Serves 3.

BAKED CHERRY TOMATOES

Eye appeal for a buffet table

cherry tomatoes--36, ripe
salt--1 teaspoon
butter (or margarine)--3 tablespoons
garlic--1 clove, crushed
pepper--1/8 teaspoon
chives--1 tablespoon

Pour boiling water over tomatoes and skin them. Sprinkle with teaspoon salt and let stand 15 minutes. Pre-heat oven to 350°F. Melt butter in shallow oven proof dish. Add garlic and pepper. Drain tomatoes, add to butter mixture, and shake so that all are well coated. Bake for 10 minutes. Sprinkle with chives. Makes 4 servings.

EGGPLANT BAKE

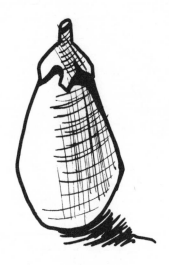

Can be cooked the day before and re-heated

        eggplant--1-1/2 lbs.
        oil--2 tablespoons
        onion--1 large, diced
        tomato sauce--16 oz. can
        tomatoes--16 oz. can
        salt--1/2 teaspoon
        pepper--1/8 teaspoon
        oregano--1/2 teaspoon
        cottage cheese--1 pint, large curd
        bread crumbs--1/2 cup
        Parmesan cheese--2 tablespoons

Peel eggplant and cut into 1" cubes. In a heavy Dutch oven,
heat oil. Fry eggplant and onion until golden brown. Add
tomato sauce, tomatoes, and seasonings. Simmer 45 minutes
or until eggplant is tender. Add cottage cheese and bread
crumbs. Place in casserole. Sprinkle with Parmesan cheese.
Bake at 350°F for 30 minutes.

Serves 8.

from fillet to flanken

CHINESE BEEF

My Malaysian friend taught me how to make this dish

        sugar--1 tablespoon
        soy sauce--4 tablespoons
        monosodium glutamate--1/4 teaspoon
        fresh ginger--1 tablespoon, mashed
        white wine--5 tablespoons
        tender beef--1 lb., sliced very thin
        fresh green beans--1 lb., cut in 2" lengths
        oil--1/4 cup
        cornstarch--1 tablespoon
        water--1/4 cup
        green onions--1/4 cup, 1" slices

Mix sugar, soy sauce, monosodium glutamate, ginger, and
wine together. Marinate meat in this sauce for 20 minutes.
Cut beans lengthwise, French style. Fry beans in oil, stirring constantly, for 2 minutes. Do not allow to brown.
Cover pan and allow to sit without heat for 5 minutes. Remove beans from pan. Add meat and stir fry until meat is
no longer red, about 3 minutes. Mix cornstarch with water.
Add to marinade. Return beans to pot. Cover with marinade.
Add green onions. Stir for 2 minutes. Remove from heat.
Cover 5 minutes. Serve immediately. Good with rice. You
may garnish with water cress.   Serves 3.

FEAST ORIENTAL

A new way to use skirt steak

    skirt steak--2 lbs., skinned, cut into bite size pieces
    tomato juice--1 cup
    pineapple juice--1/2 cup (use juice from chunks)
    soy sauce--1 tablespoon
    celery salt--1/2 teaspoon
    salt--1/4 teaspoon
    pepper--1/16 teaspoon
    brown sugar--2 tablespoons
    cornstarch--2 tablespoons
    water--3 tablespoons
    pineapple--8 oz. can, chunks, drained
    mandarin orange slices--11 oz., drained
    celery--1/2 stalk, cut into 1/2" pieces

74

Combine tomato juice, pineapple juice, soy sauce, celery salt, salt, pepper, and brown sugar. Mix well. Pour over meat and simmer covered, 30 minutes, or until tender. Combine cornstarch with cold water. Mix until smooth. Add to meat. Cook a few minutes until sauce thickens. Stir to prevent sticking. Add fruit and celery. Heat through. Serve immediately. Nice over rice. Serves 6.

BOEUF AUX FINES HERBES

Mouth watering good

boneless chuck or shin--1-1/2 lbs., cut into 2" squares
flour--2 tablespoons
salt--1/2 teaspoon
pepper--1/16 teaspoon
strip of fat--reserved from meat for frying
bay leaves--2
parsley--3 sprigs
cloves--3 whole
beef stock--3 cups (or 3 cups water and 3 bouillon cubes)
Worcestershire sauce--1/2 tablespoon
thyme--3/8 teaspoon
ketchup--3 tablespoons
garlic--1 clove, minced
potatoes--2 large, cut in wedges
yellow onions--2 large, sliced
celery--1 cup, diced
carrots--6 small, cut in 1" rounds

Dredge meat in flour, salt, and pepper. Fry strip of fat from meat in bottom of large pressure cooker. Add floured meat and fry until brown. Tie bay leaves, parsley, and cloves in piece of cheesecloth. Add this with stock, Worcestershire sauce, thyme, ketchup, and garlic to meat. Cook at 15 lbs. pressure for 15 minutes. Place cooker under cold running water and remove lid. Add vegetables and continue to cook at 15 lbs. pressure for another 3 minutes.

If you do not have a pressure cooker, bake meat covered at 350°F for 2 hours. Put in vegetables and bake 1 more hour.

Put meat and vegetables in serving dish. Add 1 tablespoon flour to thicken sauce, if necessary. Pour sauce over stew. Serves 5.

STEPHADO

A Greek stew

```
beef--chuck, 2 lbs.
olive oil--2 tablespoons
garlic--2 cloves
whole cloves--6
bay leaf--1
cinnamon--1 stick
salt--1 teaspoon
allspice--1 tablespoon, powdered
tomato juice--1 cup
ketchup--1/4 cup
red wine--1 cup
pearl onions--10 oz.
```

Trim tough fibers and fat off the meat. Cut into about 8 pieces. Brown meat well in the oil. Cut the garlic cloves in half. Tie all of the whole spices including the garlic in a clean piece of cheesecloth. Place meat in a medium size casserole. Add the spice bag, salt, allspice, tomato juice, ketchup, and wine. Bake at 350°F covered for 1-1/2 hours. Add onions and cook 30 minutes longer. Serve with rice.

Serves 4.

76

FONDUE WITH MEAT

Fork and dips

very tender beef--2 lbs., cut in 1" cubes (or very fresh
                    ground beef formed into 1" balls)
oil--1 cup
chives--1/2 cup, chopped
coarse ground pepper--1/2 tablespoon
salt--2 tablespoons
sweet and sour sauce--4 oz. jar
red cocktail sauce--4 oz. jar
bearnaise sauce--1/2 cup

Put about 8 oz. of meat and a small mound of each of the
other ingredients on each of 4 plates. Heat oil in fondue
pot or electric frying pan. Give each guest a long handled
fork so he can cook his meat in the hot oil. He then re-
moves the meat from the cooking fork, picks up meat with
another fork and dips it in condiments before devouring.

Serves 4.

A piece of dry bread dropped in hot oil will keep down
splattering.

GLAZED CORNED BEEF

Grandchildren love this, especially on picnics

corned beef--4 to 5 lbs.
margarine--2 tablespoons
ketchup--5 tablespoons
prepared mustard--1 tablespoon
white vinegar--3 tablespoons
brown sugar--1/3 cup

Place corned beef in large pot and cover with cold water.
Bring to boil and simmer until tender, usually 3 to 4 hours.
Drain and chill in refrigerator. Slice and place in large
casserole. Combine margarine, ketchup, mustard, vinegar,
and sugar in a saucepan. Bring to a boil. Pour over meat.
Bake uncovered at 350°F for 30 minutes until brown. Baste
occasionally. Serves 8.

BEEF STROGANOFF

Good for New Year's Eve or any large party

    margarine--1/2 cup
    onions--1-1/2 cups, finely chopped
    fresh mushrooms--1 lb., sliced
    top round--3-1/2 lbs., 1/2" x 1/2" x 2" strips
    flour--6 tablespoons
    bouillon--2 cups
    dried onions--1 tablespoon
    salt--1 teaspoon
    tomato paste--6 tablespoons
    sugar--1/16 teaspoon
    Worcestershire sauce--2 teaspoons
    non-dairy sour cream--1/2 pint (1 cup)
    non-dairy whipping cream--1 cup

Melt 1/4 cup margarine in large saucepan. Add onions and
saute until golden. Add mushrooms and saute until lightly
browned. Set aside.

Dredge meat in flour. Melt 1/4 cup margarine in skillet.
Saute meat until browned. Add bouillon, dried onions, and
salt. Cover. Simmer until tender about 1-1/2 hours. Cool.

Mix tomato paste, sugar, Worcestershire sauce, sour cream,
and whipping cream. Add to beef mixture. Add mushrooms
and onions to beef mixture. Heat thoroughly. Thicken with
more flour, if necessary. Serve over rice. Serves 8.

LIVER STROGANOFF

Can be served on toothpicks as hors d'oeuvres

    chicken livers--1 lb.
    onion soup mix--1 pkg. (1 to 1-1/2 oz.)
    non-dairy sour cream--1 cup
    chicken fat--2 tablespoons
    sherry wine--2 tablespoons

Fry liver in fat until done. Be careful not to overcook.
Mix onion soup, cream, and wine. Add to liver. Simmer a
few minutes to heat. Overcooking will curdle cream.
Serve with buttered noodles as an entree. Serves 3 to 4.

MILWAUKEE BRISKET

Such delicious gravy deserves fresh baked challah

```
brisket--5 to 6 lbs.
onion soup mix--1 to 1-1/2 oz. envelope
water--2 cups
ketchup--1 cup
beer--1/2 cup
flour--1/4 cup
```

Mix onion soup mix with water in the roasting pan. Season meat with salt and pepper if desired (I didn't). Place meat in pot, cover, and cook at 325°F for 2-1/2 hours or until almost done. Remove meat to cool. Pour gravy in a bowl and place in freezer. When fat hardens, remove it. Mix gravy with ketchup, beer, and flour. Slice meat, place it in roaster, add gravy mixture, and cover. Bake at 325°F for 40 minutes or until meat is tender. Excellent for buffet. I made the meat ahead of time, covered it with the gravies, and froze it before cooking it the last 40 minutes. Of course, it must be thawed before cooking.

Serves 10.

HADASSAH CHILI

A good Hadassah luncheon standby

onions--2 medium, chopped
celery--2 stalks, diced
oil--2 tablespoons
ground meat--2 lbs.
mushrooms--1/2 cup, canned
stewed tomatoes--28 oz. can
tomato soup--2 cans (10-1/2 oz. each)
water--1 cup, boiling
chili powder--3 tablespoons
sugar--1 tablespoon
salt--1-1/2 teaspoons
red kidney beans--4 cups (2 cans)

Fry onions and celery in oil until golden. Add meat and
mushrooms to pan and continue frying. Stir with fork and
break up meat as it fries. Cook slowly for 10 minutes.
Add tomatoes, tomato soup, water, sugar, and spices. Simmer
for 1 hour, uncovered. Stir occasionally to prevent
sticking.

Add kidney beans and cook another 15 minutes. Serve with a
crisp green salad.

Serves 15.

CUBED BEEF CASSEROLE

Old fashioned Chuzar style

round steak--2 lbs., 1/2" cubes
oil--3 tablespoons
onion--1 large, chopped
garlic--1 clove, crushed
celery--1/2 cup, chopped
fresh mushrooms--1/4 lb.
non-dairy sour cream--1/2 pint (1 cup)
tomato sauce--8 oz. can
flour--2 tablespoons
water--2 tablespoons
salt--1 teaspoon
pepper--1/8 teaspoon
Worcestershire sauce--1 tablespoon

Brown meat cubes with oil in a large Dutch oven. Add onions, garlic, celery, and mushrooms. Cook about 5 minutes.

Mix sour cream with tomato sauce, flour, water, salt, pepper, and Worcestershire sauce. Add to meat.

Bake at 325°F for 1 hour until tender. Nice over rice.

Serves 4.

SWEET AND SOUR TONGUE

```
tongue--about 5 lbs., fresh
onion--1 large, sliced
tomatoes--16 oz. can
lemon juice--3 tablespoons
honey--2 tablespoons
brown sugar--2 tablespoons
salt--1/2 teaspoon
allspice--1/4 teaspoon
clove--1 whole
bay leaf--1
garlic--1 clove
cinnamon--1/8 teaspoon
cold water--3 cups
raisins--3/4 cup
```

Wash tongue with a small brush. Place in a large pot and allow 1 teaspoon of salt for each quart of water. Cover completely with water and bring to a boil. Simmer for 1 hour. Remove tongue and plunge into cold water to remove skin.

Combine water, lemon juice, honey, sugar, salt, and spices to make sauce. Place sliced onions, tomatoes, and tongue in heavy pan. Add sauce. Cook until almost tender.

Remove tongue and cool. Remove bay leaf and clove. Strain sauce; then press onions and tomatoes through a sieve. Slice tongue and return to pot. Pour in sauce and add raisins. Heat thoroughly.

Serves 6.

"She hath prepared her meats, she hath mingled her wine; she hath also furnished her table." (Proverbs)

MEAT BALL VARIATIONS

Basic recipe for 1 lb. ground meat

ground meat--1 lb.
egg--1 large
onion--1/2 cup, minced
garlic--1/2 clove, crushed
salt--1/2 teaspoon
pepper--1/16 teaspoon
tomato juice--1/2 cup
cracker crumbs--2 tablespoons (bread crumbs, grated potato,
                or instant rice may be substituted)

Combine the above ingredients and form into 1-1/2" balls.

STROGANOFF SAUCE

For double meat ball basic recipe

oil--3 tablespoons
tomatoes--2 cups, canned
green pepper--2 tablespoons, chopped
non-dairy sour cream--1 cup

Brown meat balls in oil. Cover with stewed tomatoes and
green peppers. Simmer 30 minutes. Slowly mix sauce into
sour cream. Pour sauce back over meat balls. Heat through
but do not boil. Serve immediately. Nice over wild rice.

MANIC DEPRESSIVE SAUCE

onion--1 medium, chopped
olive oil--3 tablespoons
tomato soup--10-1/2 oz. can
tomato sauce--8 oz. can
water--1/2 cup
brown sugar--1 tablespoon
garlic salt--1/8 teaspoon
pepper--1/8 teaspoon
lemon juice--1 teaspoon

Saute onions in oil.

Mix tomato soup, tomato sauce, 1/2 cup water, sauteed onions, sugar, and seasonings. Cook until mixture simmers, stirring occasionally. Drop in meat balls a few at a time. Simmer 1 hour. Add lemon juice; stir and pour in your chafing dish for serving.

To use this recipe with basic meat balls, add 2 tablespoons brown sugar and 1 tablespoon lemon juice to each 2 lbs. of meat. Serves 10 to 12.

SWEET AND SOUR SAUCE

For three times the basic meat ball recipe

onions--2 medium, sliced
oil--2 tablespoons
seasoned salt--1 teaspoon
ketchup--3 tablespoons
tomato sauce--15 oz. can
brown sugar--1/3 cup
white vinegar--1/3 cup
grape jelly--2 tablespoons
Worcestershire sauce--1/8 teaspoon
water--1 cup

Fry sliced onions in oil. Add seasoned salt, ketchup, tomato sauce, brown sugar, vinegar, grape jelly, and Worcestershire sauce. Mix well. Add water and cook over low flame 30 minutes. Drop balls in the sauce and simmer for 45 minutes.

To be used for hors d'oeuvres.

BUSY DAY SAUCE

For one basic meat ball recipe

ketchup--1 cup
Worcestershire sauce--1 tablespoon
vinegar--2 tablespoons
salt--1/4 teaspoon
pepper--1/8 teaspoon
brown sugar--2 tablespoons
onion--2 tablespoons, instant minced

Place meat balls in 2 quart casserole.

Mix all ingredients to make sauce. Pour sauce over meat balls and bake at 350°F for 1 hour. Good over buttered noodles.

Serves 4.

FRUITED MEAT SAUCE

For double meat ball basic recipe

cranberries--16 oz. can
salt--1/2 teaspoon
pepper--1/16 teaspoon
chili sauce--10 oz.

In large saucepan, mix together cranberries, seasoning, and chili sauce. Bring to a boil. Drop in meat balls. Lower to simmer and cook covered for 35 minutes. Stir frequently to prevent burning. Uncover and cook 15 minutes longer.

Serves 10.

CABBAGE ROLLS

For one meat ball basic recipe

To prepare stuffed cabbage, use 1 large head (approximately 12 leaves). Wash cabbage; cut out core. Cook in boiling water for 10 minutes. Drain well. Separate leaves carefully to keep whole. Divide meat into 12 parts and place mixture on each cabbage leaf. Tuck the opposite sides in and carefully roll up the cabbage leaf.

TOMATO SAUCE

FOR CABBAGE ROLLS

For one meat ball basic recipe

    onion--1 large, minced
    oil--2 tablespoons
    salt--1/2 teaspoon
    paprika--1/4 teaspoon
    pepper--1/16 teaspoon
    hot water--1/2 cup
    tomato sauce--2 cans (8 oz. each)
    lemon juice--1/4 cup
    sugar--1/4 to 1/2 cup

Saute minced onion in oil with salt, paprika, and pepper
until onions are tender. Add hot water; put cabbage rolls
on top of onion. Mix tomato sauce, lemon juice, and sugar.
Pour over rolls. Cook over low heat 1-1/2 hours or bake at
325°F for 2 hours. Add more sugar and lemon juice if
needed. You may freeze stuffed cabbage.

GINGER SAUCE

FOR CABBAGE ROLLS

For one meat ball basic recipe

```
onion--1 small, chopped
oil--1 tablespoon
tomato sauce--2 cans (8 oz. each)
whole cranberries--16 oz. can
ginger snaps--4 crumbled
water--1/4 cup
```

Saute onion in oil. Add tomato sauce and cranberries.
Cook 5 minutes. Crumble ginger snaps in a separate dish
and cover with water until dissolved. Add to sauce. Cook
stuffed cabbage covered in sauce 1-1/2 hours over low flame.
Serve.

VEAL GOULASH

A flavorful stew

```
veal shoulder or veal stew--1-1/2 lbs., boned
oil--3 tablespoons
salt--3/4 teaspoon
onions--1 cup, sliced
vinegar--5 tablespoons, or to taste
caraway seed--1 teaspoon
water--1-1/2 cups
paprika--1-1/2 teaspoons
marjoram--1 teaspoon
flour--1 tablespoon
water--1/4 cup, cold
```

Cut veal into 2" cubes. Heat oil in deep skillet or Dutch
oven. Brown veal on all sides in hot oil and sprinkle with
salt. Add onions and cook until lightly browned, stirring
constantly. Add vinegar, caraway seeds, and 1-1/2 cups
water. Cover. Simmer 30 minutes, then add paprika and
marjoram. Cover. Simmer 30 minutes more or until tender.
If liquid boils down you may add more hot water. Taste.
Add more salt if needed.

Blend flour with 1/4 cup water. Stir into goulash and cook
until thickened and continue stirring. Good with buttered
noodles or fluffy white rice. Serves 4.

SPANISH TONGUE

May be used as a snack with drinks

        tongue--3 to 4 lbs., fresh
        salt--1 teaspoon for each quart of water
        pepper--1/8 teaspoon
        garlic--1 whole cluster, unpeeled
        oil--6 tablespoons
        onions--2 medium, sliced
        celery--1 small bunch, diced
        tomato soup--2 cans (11 oz. each)
        peas--17 oz. can, drained
        mushroom buttons--4 oz. can

Scrub tongue with a small brush. Place tongue in pot and
cover with cold water. Add salt, pepper, and garlic. Simmer covered 3 to 4 hours or until tender. Take out of pot
and plunge into cold water. Remove skin and cut away roots.
Cut tongue into 1" squares. Heat oil in frying pan. Add
onions and cook until golden. Add celery and cook until
tender. Add soup; mix thoroughly. Add tongue. Mix and
simmer 20 minutes. Add peas and mushrooms and stir as it
heats. Nice with rice. Serves 6 to 8.

GLAZED LAMB KABOBS

        onion--1 large, chopped fine
        meat marinade--1 envelope (instant)
        apple-apricot baby food--2 jars, strained
        water--1/2 cup
        lamb shoulder or leg--2 lbs., boned, cut in 1" cubes
        mushrooms--8 large
        cherry tomatoes--8
        green pepper--cut into 8 pieces
        pineapple chunks--8

Blend meat marinade thoroughly with apple-apricots, onion,
and water in a shallow dish. Place lamb cubes in dish,
pierce all over with a fork. Let stand, turning meat every
15 minutes. Thread lamb chunks, whole mushrooms, cherry
tomatoes, green pepper and pineapple chunks onto skewers.
Place on rack in broiler pan, as close to heat as possible,
turning and basting several times with remaining marinade
in dish. Continue for 10 minutes or until lamb is tender
and richly glazed. Also good on barbecue. Serves 6.

PESACH SPAGHETTI

It's really good

Dough:

egg--1 large
water--1/2 cup
salt--1 teaspoon
pepper--1/4 teaspoon
matzo meal--1 cup, sifted
boiling water--2 quarts (add 2 teaspoons salt)

Meat Balls:

ground beef--1 lb.
egg--1 large
onion--1 small, minced
salt--1/2 teaspoon
pepper--1/8 teaspoon
matzo meal--2 tablespoons
water--3 tablespoons
peanut oil--3 tablespoons
tomato mushroom sauce for Passover--10-1/2 oz. can

Mix egg, 1/2 cup water, salt, and pepper together with a rotary beater. Gradually stir in matzo meal. Cover and chill overnight. Take a piece of dough the size of a green pea and roll out pencil fashion between palm of hand and a flat clean surface, (such as a rolling board) as long and thin as possible. I found if I used wax paper it made it easier. You may also lightly coat hands with a little shortening if you find it easier. Place on flat plate until ready to use. Add to 2 quarts boiling water and cook 20 minutes. Drain well.

While this is cooking, combine all remaining ingredients except oil and tomato mushroom sauce. (This is now being sold in the markets for Passover.) Dampen hands and shape into about 16 balls.

Heat oil and brown meat balls quickly. Add tomato mushroom sauce. Cover and cook 15 minutes, turning at least once.

Serve on Pesach spaghetti, and you really have something different for Passover.

Serves 4.

CUTLETS STROGANOFF

Good and easy

        veal cutlets--4 large
        egg--1 large, beaten
        bread crumbs--4 tablespoons
        oil--1 tablespoon
        mushroom steak sauce--5-3/4 oz. can
        non-dairy sour cream--1/2 pint (1 cup)

Dip veal in egg. Then coat with bread crumbs. Fry in oil
until lightly browned. Remove to bottom of baking dish.
Mix steak sauce and sour cream together. Pour over cutlets.
Cover. Bake at 350°F for 1 hour. Serve over rice.

EAST WEST DELIGHT

A Geoff Edwards' award winner in 1971 Lawry's cook off

        ground beef--1 lb.
        oil--2 tablespoons
        fresh chop suey vegetables--16 oz. package
        fresh mushrooms--1/4 lb., sliced
        water chestnuts--3 oz. can, drained and sliced
        brown gravy mix--1 pkg., 1-1/2 oz.
        water--1-1/4 cups
        prepared mustard--2 tablespoons
        soy sauce--2 tablespoons
        ketchup--1 tablespoon
        garlic--2 cloves, crushed
        seasoning salt--1 teaspoon
        tomatoes--2 medium, skinned and cut in wedges
        rice--3 cups, cooked
        almonds--2 oz., toasted, slivered
        chow mein noodles--3 oz. can

Brown ground beef without oil. Stir with a fork to break
up pieces and to keep meat from sticking. Remove meat from
pan. Add oil to same pan. Heat. Add chop suey vegetables,
mushrooms, and water chestnuts. Stir. Cover and cook 3 minutes. Combine gravy mix, water, mustard, soy sauce, ketchup,
garlic, and seasoning salt. Stir meat into the vegetables.
Add gravy and tomato wedges. Cover and simmer 4 minutes.
Do not overcook vegetables. Serve over rice. Top with almonds and chow mein noodles. Serves 6.

MOUSAKA

I learned to make this when I lived in Greece

         artichoke hearts--12 oz., drained
         onions--1 cup, diced
         olive oil--2 tablespoons
         ground chuck--2 lbs.
         salt--1 teaspoon
         garlic salt--1/2 teaspoon
         pepper--1/2 teaspoon
         oregano--1/2 teaspoon
         tomatoes--8 oz. can
         ketchup--2 tablespoons
         margarine--1/2 cup
         flour--1/2 cup
         non-dairy milk--1 quart
         bouillon cubes--2
         eggs--2 large

Line bottom of 3 quart casserole with well drained artichoke hearts. Fry onions in olive oil. Add meat and
seasonings and continue to fry. Stir occasionally to break
up meat and to fry evenly. Fry only until meat is no longer red. Add tomatoes and ketchup. Continue to cook for 10
more minutes. Pour over the artichokes. Melt margarine.
Add flour. Remove from heat. Stir in a little of the
milk to make a paste. Gradually add the rest of the milk.
Do not allow flour to lump. Return to heat and cook until
thick. Remove from heat. Crumble in bouillon cubes. Beat
in eggs one at a time, making a thick paste.

Spread over meat in casserole. Bake at 350°F for 25 minutes. Do not overcook. (Fried eggplant slices may be substituted for the artichoke hearts.) Serves 8.

YUMMY MEAT LOAF

A family favorite

        ground beef--1-1/2 lbs.
        bread crumbs--1/2 cup
        egg--1 large
        onion--1 medium, grated
        salt--1 teaspoon
        pepper--1/4 teaspoon
        tomato sauce--8 oz. can
        white vinegar--2 tablespoons
        brown sugar--2 tablespoons
        mustard--2 tablespoons, prepared

Mix meat, bread crumbs, egg, onion, seasonings, and half of
tomato sauce together. Form into a loaf and bake at 350°F
for 1 hour. While meat is cooking, mix the other half of
tomato sauce with the vinegar, brown sugar, and mustard.
Heat until sugar is all dissolved. Baste meat often with
the sauce during the cooking. Sauce should be all used up
when meat is done. Serves 4.

CHOLENT

This was originally made to cook
slowly for 24 hours on Shabbat

        dried lima beans--1/2 lb.
        brisket--4 to 6 lbs.
        salt--1-1/2 teaspoons
        pepper--1/4 teaspoon
        dry mustard--1/4 teaspoon
        garlic salt--1/4 teaspoon
        tomato juice--1 quart
        onions--2 medium, sliced
        dried apricots--1/2 lb.
        water--1 cup

Soak lima beans overnight in 3 quarts of water. Wipe meat
dry and season with salt, pepper, mustard, and garlic salt.
Place in roasting pan. Line lima beans on either side of
meat. Add tomato juice. Cover meat with onions. Bake in
350°F oven 3 to 4 hours or until tender. Turn regularly.
Add dried apricots and water. Cook another 30 minutes.
Serves 10.

HADASSAH CHOW MEIN

Your family will like this too

    onions--2 medium (2 cups), chopped
    green pepper--1/2 medium, diced
    celery--1 cup, sliced
    oil--1/4 cup
    ground beef--2 lbs.
    quick brown rice--1/4 cup
    garlic--1 clove, crushed
    salt--1 teaspoon
    pepper--1/8 teaspoon
    kasha soup--10-1/2 oz. can
    non-dairy sour cream--1/2 cup
    French fried onions--3-1/2 oz. can

Saute onions, pepper, and celery in oil until lightly browned. Add rice and fry with vegetables for a few minutes. Add the meat, stirring constantly, breaking up meat as it fries. Add garlic, salt, pepper, soup, and sour cream. Mix well.

Put into 10" x 13" baking dish. Cover with foil. Bake at 350°F for 1 hour. Cover with the onions. Bake 5 minutes. Nice with Chinese fried noodles.

Serves 10.

TURKISH EGGPLANT

A different and tasty way to serve eggplant

    eggplant--1-1/2 lbs.
    onion--1 medium, chopped
    oil--4 tablespoons
    tomato sauce--1-1/4 cups
    mint leaves--2 teaspoons, chopped
    dill seed--2 teaspoons
    salt--1 teaspoon
    pepper--1/16 teaspoon
    ground beef--1 lb.
    water--1/4 cup
    margarine--1 teaspoon

Wash eggplant. Slice in half the long way. Scoop out flesh with a sharp knife. The shells should be 1/2" thick.

Dice eggplant. Saute in oil with onions. Add tomato sauce, mint leaves, dill, salt, pepper, and ground beef. Mix thoroughly. Fill shells with mixture.

Coat baking dish with margarine. Put in water. Place filled shells in the water. Cover baking dish with foil. Bake at 350°F for 1 hour. Serves 6.

For real Turkish style, use ground lamb.

TOMATO NOODLE CASSEROLE

Cuts into perfect squares

oil--3 tablespoons
ground beef--1 lb.
onions--2 medium, diced
garlic clove--1, minced
tomatoes--29 oz. can
tomato paste--6 oz. can
water--3/4 cup (or dry wine)
salt--2 teaspoons
paprika--1/2 teaspoon
thyme--1/8 teaspoon
marjoram--1/8 teaspoon
bay leaf--1
Worcestershire sauce--1 teaspoon
tabasco--1/8 teaspoon
noodles--8 oz., wide, uncooked

This recipe should be prepared in the morning and refriger-ated until ready to heat. Heat oil in a heavy skillet. Add meat, breaking into small pieces with fork. Add onions and garlic. When meat is brown, add tomatoes, tomato paste, and water or wine. Bring to a boil; then add salt, paprika, thyme, marjoram, bay leaf, Worcestershire sauce, and tabasco. Simmer for a few minutes until flavors are combined. Remove bay leaf. Place half the sauce into a 3 quart casserole. Add uncooked noodles and pour remaining sauce on top.

Cover and refrigerate. Bake covered in moderate oven, 375°F, for 45 minutes.

Serves 6.

PRINCE SCALLOPINI

Nice enough for company

```
veal--1 lb., sliced thin
flour--4 tablespoons
salt--1/2 teaspoon
pepper--1/16 teaspoon
olive oil--3 tablespoons
onion--1 small, chopped
mushrooms--1/2 cup, sliced
green onions--3 tablespoons, chopped
white wine--1/2 cup
bouillon cube--1
tomato juice--3/4 cup
garlic--1 clove, crushed
rosemary--1/2 teaspoon
tarragon--1/8 teaspoon
vinegar--1 tablespoon
```

Pound veal well. Mix flour, salt, and pepper. Dredge meat in flour. Fry in oil until brown. Remove meat from pan and set aside.

Place onion, mushrooms, and green onions into pan used for frying meat. Fry until lightly brown. Add remaining ingredients. Simmer sauce for 10 minutes.

Return veal to sauce. Cover and continue cooking for about 1 hour or until meat is tender.

Watch during cooking to be sure meat is always covered with sauce. Add more water if needed.

Serve over noodles.

A few sprigs of parsley make a nice garnish for this dish.

Serves 3.

****

"Behold, I have given you every herb yielding seed, which is upon the face of all the earth, and every tree in which is the fruit of a tree yielding seed--to you it shall be for food." (Genesis)

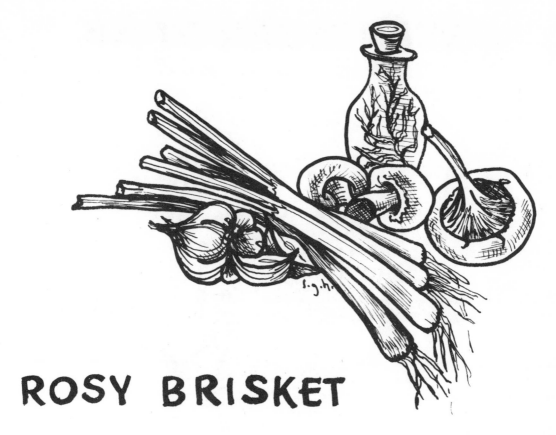

ROSY BRISKET

Brisket par excellence

    beef brisket--4 to 5 lbs., first cut
    salt--1 teaspoon
    pepper--1/8 teaspoon
    onions--2 large, sliced
    garlic--1 clove, crushed
    brown sugar--1/2 lb., light brown
    orange juice--1/2 cup
    flour--1 tablespoon

Season brisket with salt and pepper. Rub with garlic.
Line baking dish with sliced onions. Place meat on top of
onions. Pack well top and sides of meat with brown sugar
to keep in juices as no cover is used.

Bake at 275°F for 4 hours or until tender. Cover dish with
foil and chill. Remove congealed fat. Cut meat in thin
slices. Add orange juice and flour to juice to make gravy.
Reheat. Check to be sure gravy thickens before removing.
If you prefer a smooth sauce you may blend or puree onions.
Nice with mashed potatoes. Serves 8.

95

LIVER–ITALIAN STYLE

High source of iron

flour--3 tablespoons
pepper--1/8 teaspoon
salt--1/4 teaspoon
calves liver--1 lb., sliced
margarine--3 tablespoons
lemon juice--3 tablespoons
lemon rind--1/2 teaspoon, grated
thyme--1/2 teaspoon

Mix flour with salt and pepper. Dredge liver in flour.
Fry in 2 tablespoons of the margarine until slightly pink
when cut. Remove from pan. Add 1 tablespoon of margarine
to pan. Add lemon juice and grated rind. Add thyme if
desired. Thyme disguises the liver flavor.

Pour sauce over liver and serve.

LIVER BLINTZES

A great Passover dish

<u>Leaves</u>:

eggs--3 large
salt--1/2 teaspoon
water--1-1/2 cups
matzo cake meal--2/3 cup

Combine eggs, salt, and water. Add cake meal gradually, stirring constantly and thoroughly to avoid lumps. In a hot, lightly greased frying pan pour about 3 tablespoons of batter and rotate pan so batter forms a 6" circle. Fry over moderate heat until edges pull away from pan. Turn out on a clean cloth, cooked side up. Repeat until all the batter is used.

<u>Filling</u>:

onions--2 large, minced
chicken fat or oil--1/2 cup
liver--1-1/2 lbs.
egg--1 large, slightly beaten
salt--1 teaspoon
white pepper--1/8 teaspoon
tomato mushroom sauce--2 cans (10-1/2 oz. each)

Saute onions in chicken fat or oil until golden. Place liver on top of onions. Cover and cook only until pink is gone, turning once. Grind liver and onions. Add egg, salt, and pepper and mix well. Place a heaping tablespoon of this filling in the center of each leaf. Fold in side edges and roll tightly. Fry until golden brown in a small amount of chicken fat or oil.

Heat tomato mushroom sauce and serve separately as sauce for blintzes.

Makes 14 to 16 blintzes.

****

"Spikenard and saffron, calamus and cinnamon, myrrh and aloes, with all the chief spices." (Song of Songs)

97

ARMENIAN LAMB STEW

American twist on an Armenian dish

onion--1 large, chopped
garlic--2 cloves, minced
oil--6 tablespoons
lamb--1-1/2 lbs., boneless, cut in 2" cubes
tomato paste--1/4 cup
bouillon--1-1/2 cups
oregano--1 teaspoon
salt--1/4 teaspoon
pepper--1/8 teaspoon
finger eggplant--1-1/2 lbs.
lemon juice--1 tablespoon

Cook onions and garlic in 3 tablespoons of oil until onion is transparent. Add meat and cook until meat is lightly browned. Mix tomato paste, bouillon, oregano, salt and pepper. Stir into meat mixture. Simmer covered 1-1/4 hours. Cut eggplant into 1/2" horizontal slices. Cook in remaining oil until lightly browned, but firm. Add to meat and cook 20 minutes longer. Sprinkle with lemon juice just before serving. Very good with brown rice.

Serves 4.

LAMB INDONESIAN

You'd never guess it was "used" lamb

lamb--1-1/2 lbs, cooked and sliced thin
soy sauce--1/2 cup
garlic--1 clove, crushed
dill weed--1/2 teaspoon
sugar--1 tablespoon
lemon juice--3 tablespoons
olive oil--1/4 cup

Mix all ingredients except lamb in a sauce pan. Bring to a boil. Marinate lamb in sauce for 1 hour. Remove lamb from sauce and broil under high heat or on barbecue, brushing often with sauce. Cook a few minutes on each side.

Serves 4.

from kotchKe to carp

TANTE'S GEFILTE FISH

I'm sure you have an aunt who made it just like this

pike--3/4 lb.
Eastern white fish--3/4 lb.
carp--1/4 lb.
onions--1-1/2 large
carrot--1 large, sliced
salt--1 teaspoon
white pepper--1/8 teaspoon
egg--1 large
cold water--4 quarts

Ask your fish man
to filet your fish
and grind it.

Place fish head, skin, and bones in
bottom of soup pot. Add 1 whole onion and carrots to pot.
Add water and bring to a boil. Continue to boil (at least
30 minutes) while you prepare fish. Force 1/2 onion
through a meat grinder, or chop a small amount at a time in
a blender on slow speed.

Combine fish with onions, eggs, salt, and pepper. Form
fish into 2" balls. Remove skin and bones from bottom of
pot. Drop fish balls into rapidly boiling water. If necessary, add just enough water to cover fish. Cover pot and
cook slowly for 2-1/2 hours until stock has been reduced to
less than half. Remove fish to a platter and pour the
strained fish stock over it. Refrigerate overnight until
the stock jells. Best with fresh horseradish. Serves 6.

100

TUNA ORIENTA

A favorite luncheon dish

    brown sugar--3 tablespoons
    soy sauce--1 tablespoon
    cornstarch--2-1/2 tablespoons
    white vinegar--2 tablespoons
    onion soup mix--1/2 envelope (approximately 2/3 oz.)
    pineapple juice--1 cup
    butter--2 tablespoons
    green pepper--1 large, diced
    celery--1 cup, diced
    tuna--2 cans (7 oz. each), drained
    pineapple tid-bits--15 oz. can, drained
    water chestnuts--6 oz. can, drained
    bean sprouts--16 oz. can, drained
    Chinese noodles--3 oz. can
    slivered almonds--1 oz.

In large saucepan combine sugar, soy sauce, cornstarch, vinegar, soup mix, and pineapple juice. Cook until thick. Slightly saute in butter, green pepper and celery. Add with tuna, pineapple tid-bits, water chestnuts, and bean sprouts to thickened mixture. Warm through. Serve on rice or Chinese noodles, or both, and top with slivered almonds.

TUNA RICE CASSEROLE

Well received at a Hadassah Board luncheon

    milk--1-1/4 cups
    cream of mushroom soup--2 cans (10-1/2 oz. each)
    chopped black olives--2-1/4 oz. can
    tuna--13 oz. can, flaked
    rice--2-1/2 cups, cooked firm
    Chinese hard noodles--5 oz. can
    cheddar cheese or American--4 oz., grated

Add milk, soup, and olives to tuna in a saucepan. Heat. Add rice. Place mixture in a greased 3 quart baking dish. Cover with Chinese noodles. Sprinkle with cheddar cheese. Bake at 375°F for 35 minutes. Uncover. Bake for 5 minutes.

Serves 6.

BAKED TROUT

A welcome change from meat

    fresh mushrooms--1/2 lb., sliced
    butter--6 tablespoons
    lemon juice--1 teaspoon
    trout--1-1/2 to 2 lbs., (approximately 4 small, whole)
    salt--1/2 teaspoon
    pepper--1/4 teaspoon
    flour--2 tablespoons
    olive oil--2 tablespoons
    green onions--2, thinly sliced
    coarse bread crumbs--1/4 cup

Fry mushrooms in 2 tablespoons of butter. Sprinkle with lemon juice. Stir almost constantly. Cook 3 minutes until they glisten with butter. Transfer to 9" x 13" baking dish.

Rub trout with salt and pepper. Roll in flour, shaking off excess. Add 2 tablespoons butter and oil to skillet. Fry 4 to 5 minutes on each side until golden brown. Arrange in single layer over the mushrooms.

Add 1 tablespoon butter to skillet. Fry green onions for 1 minute. Spread over fish.

Lightly brown bread crumbs in remaining butter in skillet. Sprinkle over fish.

Bake at 450°F for 10 minutes or until bread crumbs are golden brown.

Serve directly from baking dish. This may be prepared in advance except for baking. When you are ready to serve, bake 15 minutes instead of 10 minutes. Serves 4.

SALMON LOAF

Good for any occasion

    salmon--1 lb. can, drained, skin and bones removed
    matzo meal--2 tablespoons
    garlic powder--1/2 teaspoon
    seasoned salt--1 teaspoon
    eggs--4 large, separated
    onion--4 teaspoons, grated
    sour cream--1/2 pint (1 cup)

102

Mix the salmon, matzo meal, seasonings, and egg yolks well. Add onions and sour cream. Beat whites until stiff and carefully fold into salmon mixture. Pour into well greased casserole. Bake at 350°F, uncovered, for 45 minutes.

Nice with broccoli and potatoes. Serves 4.

CHOW MEIN

A good standby for luncheon meetings

    water--1/4 cup
    soy sauce--1 tablespoon
    mushroom soup--10-1/2 oz. can
    chow mein noodles--3 oz. can
    tuna--2 cans (7 oz. each), washed and drained
    water chestnuts--1 cup, sliced
    mushrooms--4 oz., drained, sliced
    green onions--1/4 cup, chopped
    celery--1 cup, chopped

Combine water, soy sauce, and soup. Mix in 1 cup noodles and remaining ingredients. Pour into a 2 quart greased casserole. Refrigerate for 2 hours. Sprinkle with remaining noodles. Bake uncovered at 375°F for 45 minutes.

Serves 6 to 8.

PRIZE TUNA CASSEROLE

This recipe won a prize in Chicago

    oil--2 tablespoons
    onions--2, chopped
    green pepper--1, chopped
    mushrooms--1/2 cup canned, chopped
    tuna--2 cans (7 oz. each), drained and flaked
    tomato soup--10 oz. can, undiluted
    frozen peas--10 oz. pkg., thawed
    cornflakes--1/4 cup, crumbled

Saute onions and pepper in oil until tender. Add mushrooms, tuna, tomato soup, and peas. Put into a 2 quart casserole. Cover with cornflakes. Bake at 350°F for 45 minutes.

Serves 8.

"SORRY CHARLIE" CASSEROLE

One of the best tuna recipes around

    wide egg noodles--8 oz., cooked according to directions
    French fried onions--2 cans (3-1/2 oz. each)
    tuna--3 cans (7 oz. each), drained and washed
    water chestnuts--6 oz. can, sliced
    sour cream--1/2 pint (1 cup)
    cream of mushroom soup--2 cans (10-1/2 oz. each)

Combine noodles, 1 can of onions, tuna, water chestnuts, sour cream, and soup. Put into a 3 quart buttered casserole. Place remaining onions on top and bake covered at 350°F for 25 minutes. Uncover. Bake for 5 minutes.

CHICKEN MOROCCO

A dish with a foreign flavor

    chicken fryer or broiler--2-1/2 to 3 lbs., cut up
    salt--1 teaspoon
    garlic powder--1/2 teaspoon
    pepper--1/4 teaspoon
    paprika--1/2 teaspoon
    margarine--3 tablespoons
    chicken stock--1/2 to 3/4 cup
    garlic--1 clove, crushed
    eggplant--1 medium, peeled and diced
    green onions--4, chopped
    tomatoes--2, peeled, diced
    thyme--1/4 teaspoon
    parsley--1 tablespoon, chopped

Sprinkle chicken pieces with 1/2 teaspoon salt, garlic powder, pepper, and paprika. Melt margarine in a large skillet or electric fry pan. Add chicken pieces skin side down and cook until lightly browned. Add more margarine if necessary. Remove chicken from skillet. Add stock and scrape brown particles from bottom of skillet. Add garlic, eggplant, green onions, and tomatoes. Return chicken to skillet. Sprinkle with 1/2 teaspoon salt, thyme, and parsley. Cover and simmer 30 to 45 minutes or until done. Add more chicken stock if necessary.

Good served with rice or noodles. Serves 4.

CHERRY JUBILEE CHICKEN

For your favorite company

        chicken fryer--1 large, cut up
        seasoning salt--1 teaspoon
        pitted bing cherries--1 lb. can
        cornstarch--2-1/2 teaspoons
        lemon juice--2 tablespoons
        ground cloves--1/4 teaspoon
        margarine--2 tablespoons
        brown sugar--2 tablespoons
        sherry cooking wine--2 tablespoons
        brandy--2 tablespoons

Sprinkle chicken with seasoning salt. Bake at 350°F for 1
hour. Meanwhile, combine syrup from can of cherries with
cornstarch. Cook until thick; then add lemon juice, cloves,
margarine, brown sugar, and sherry. Heat to boiling point
and pour over chicken. Pour 1 tablespoon brandy evenly
over chicken. Put 1 tablespoon brandy into a spoon; flame,
and pour over chicken. Nice served with rice and Green
Beans Almondine. Serves 3.

Serve sauce over ice cream and you have a delicious dessert.

TURKEY TREAT

Our girls thought this was too good for a luncheon meeting!

        turkey or chicken--4 cups, cooked and diced
        celery--1 cup, diced
        green onions--3 tablespoons, sliced
        almonds--3 oz., sliced
        mayonnaise--1 cup
        non-dairy sour cream--1/2 pint (1 cup)
        kasha soup--10-1/2 oz. can
        lemon juice--3 tablespoons
        potato chips--3 oz. pkg., crushed

Grease a 10" casserole dish. Mix together all ingredients,
except the potato chips. Pour into casserole and top with
potato chips. Bake at 325°F for 30 minutes. Serve with
rice.

Serves 8 to 10.

DUCK L'ORANGE

When the king comes to visit, serve this

```
duck--4 to 5 lbs.
salt--1 teaspoon

grapes--1 cup, fresh or canned
dried apricots--1/2 cup
pitted prunes--1/2 cup
apple--1 medium, peeled and sliced
almonds--1/4 lb.
port wine--1/2 cup plus 2 tablespoons

orange rind--from 1 orange
boiling water--1/2 cup
sugar--2 tablespoons
vinegar--2 tablespoons
chicken broth--1-1/4 cups

cornstarch--2 tablespoons
orange brandy--2 tablespoons
orange juice--1/2 cup
orange marmalade--3 tablespoons
```

Rub inside of cavity and outside of duck with salt.

Marinate fruit and nuts in 1/2 cup of wine for 4 hours.

Stuff cavity of duck with marinated fruit. Tie legs to tail and wings to back. Prick skin very, very well to allow the fat to seep out. Put on rack in 450°F oven for 1/2 hour. Prick well again. Chill gravy. Remove fat from basting pan.

To prepare orange sauce, pare rind from one orange. Cover with 1/2 cup boiling water. Let sit 5 minutes. Remove rind. Add sugar and vinegar. Boil in heavy pot, stirring constantly, until sauce browns just slightly or caramelizes. Remove from heat and carefully add 1/2 cup chicken broth.

Remove stuffing from duck. Cut duck into quarters. Make 4 mounds of the fruit stuffing in the roasting pan. Cover each mound with a quarter of the duck. Put back into a 350°F oven and continue baking for 90 minutes or until duck is tender. Baste every 15 minutes with orange sauce. Use half of the sauce. Run a pancake turner under each quarter of duck, lifting fruit with the duck and place on serving dish and keep warm.

Remove grease from baking pan. Mix cornstarch with 3/4 cup cold chicken broth. Add gravy left in baking pan. Add remainder of orange sauce. Cook until thick, stirring constantly. Add orange brandy, orange juice, and marmalade. Heat a few minutes. Pour half over the duck and use the other half as gravy.

Best with wild rice. Serves 2 to 3.

CRANBERRY CHICKEN

A favorite at a large buffet dinner

    frying chickens--2 (3 lbs. each), cut up
    whole cranberries--16 oz. can
    onion soup mix--1 envelope (1 oz. to 1-1/2 oz.)
    creamy French dressing--1/2 cup

Mix cranberries, soup mix, and French dressing together. Dip chicken into mixture and place on foil lined cookie sheet. Bake at 350°F for 1-1/2 hours. Serves 5.

DUCK MANDARIN STYLE

With Peking duck additions

duck--4 lb. frozen, cut into quarters
onion--1 small, diced
celery--1 stalk, chopped
salt--1 teaspoon
water--1 cup plus 3 tablespoons
fresh ginger--5 very thin slices (or 1 teaspoon ground)
garlic--1/8 teaspoon
pineapple juice--1 cup, from pineapple chunks
oil--2 tablespoons
pineapple chunks--1 lb. can, drained
green pepper--1, diced
monosodium glutamate--1/16 teaspoon
sherry wine--1/4 cup
soy sauce--3 tablespoons
cornstarch--3 tablespoons
water--3 tablespoons

Remove skin from breast, reserve for Peking Duck Sandwiches.

Separate neck, giblets, and ends of wings. Simmer in 1 cup water with onion, celery, and 1/2 teaspoon salt for 1 hour.

Mix 1/2 teaspoon salt, fresh ginger, garlic, and pineapple juice. Pour over duck. Marinate for 8 hours or more.

Remove duck from marinade and brown in Dutch oven with oil. Bake at 350°F for 1 hour. Be sure duck is tender but not separating from bone.

Strain soup made from giblets, neck, and wings. Add marinade, pineapple chunks, green pepper, monosodium glutamate, sherry wine, and soy sauce. Cook 2 minutes. Mix cornstarch with 3 tablespoons water. Add to sauce. Cook 3 minutes to thicken. Pour over duck. Serve with rice. Serves 3.

PEKING DUCK SANDWICHES

To serve with Duck Mandarin Style

raw skin from duck
green onions--6, cut into 1" pieces
Parkerhouse rolls--6, medium

Put large pieces of raw skin over a cooking rack and bake at 350°F for 1-1/2 hours or until crisp. Cut into 3" squares. Split rolls. Fill with crisp skin and green onions.

Serve these sandwiches with hot duck.   Serves 3.

COQ AU VIN

This is the real thing

    chicken fryers--2 medium, cut up
    flour--1/2 cup
    salt--1/2 teaspoon
    pepper--1/8 teaspoon
    paprika--1/2 teaspoon
    margarine--1/2 cup
    onions--4 medium, cut in eighths
    chicken broth--1 cup
    dry white wine--3 cups
    thyme, parsley, rosemary--1/4 teaspoon each
    bay leaf--1
    mushrooms--1 cup, chopped
    Madeira wine--2 tablespoons

Mix flour with salt, pepper, and paprika. Dredge chicken in seasoned flour and fry in margarine until brown. Remove chicken to casserole. Add onions to margarine and fry until barely brown. Add broth, white wine, and seasonings. Boil until mixture decreases by one half. Pour mixture over chicken; add mushrooms and bake at 350°F for about 45 minutes, or until chicken is done. Add the Madeira just before serving. Serve with rice. (Chicken may be frozen after adding sauce and may be baked later.) Serves 6.

CHICKEN VARIATION

    chicken parts--3 lbs.
    French dressing--8 oz.

Empty dressing in a 3 quart glass casserole and marinate chicken pieces in it for at least 8 hours, or overnight. Bake in same dish at 350°F for 1 hour until crispy.

CURRIED CHICKEN

Good even without the curry

    chicken fryer or favorite chicken parts--3 lbs.
    curry powder--1 teaspoon
    salt--1/2 teaspoon
    orange juice--1/2 cup
    honey--1/3 cup
    prepared mustard--1/4 teaspoon
    oranges--2

Sprinkle chicken with curry powder and salt on both sides
and rub into meat. Combine orange juice, honey, and mustard and mix until well blended. Dip chicken in marinade.
Place chicken in baking dish skin side down. Pour remaining marinade over chicken. Bake at 325°F for about 30 minutes covered. Watch to be sure chicken does not burn.
Turn chicken over so skin side is up and continue baking
for 45 minutes or until tender and richly brown. Baste
often with juices in pan. While chicken is baking, peel
oranges; slice and cut each slice in half. Remove chicken
to serving platter. Add orange to juices in pan and heat
1 minute. Serve sauce over chicken. Delicious with plain
steamed rice and raisins.

CHICKEN WHIRLS

Can be used as a main course or appetizers

    chicken breasts--3 large, boned and flattened
    egg--1 large, slightly beaten
    salt--1/2 teaspoon
    bread crumbs--1/2 cup
    sesame seeds--1/4 cup
    margarine--2 tablespoons

Cut chicken into strips. Dip each strip into egg and salt
mixture. Then dip into bread crumbs, back into egg and
then roll in sesame seeds. Roll each strip so it looks
like an anchovy roll. Thread each one onto a wooden skewer.
Fry in margarine until brown on both sides. Bake at 350°F
for 20 minutes. Makes 12 whirls.

Serves 2 for dinner.

SHERRY CHICKEN

Elegant and real easy

chicken fryers--2 (2 to 3 lbs. each), cut up (or parts)
salt--1 teaspoon
pepper--1/4 teaspoon
garlic salt--1/2 teaspoon
oil--1/4 cup
onions--1 cup, diced
celery--1 cup, chopped
fresh mushrooms--1/4 lb., sliced
non-dairy sour cream--1 pint (2 cups)
sherry wine--1/2 cup
flour--1 tablespoon
paprika--1/4 teaspoon

Sprinkle chicken with salt, pepper, and garlic salt. Place in one layer in roasting pan. Saute onions in oil until golden. Add celery and mushrooms. Saute 2 minutes. Add non-dairy sour cream, sherry, and flour. Stir. Pour over chicken. Bake uncovered at 350°F for 1-1/2 hours. Baste frequently. Sprinkle with paprika before serving.

Serves 5.

BAKED HONEY CHICKEN

A honey of a chicken

    chicken parts--3 to 4 lbs.
    honey--1/4 cup
    soy sauce--1/4 cup
    ketchup--1/2 cup
    fresh lemon juice--1/4 cup
    pineapple chunks--1 lb. can, drained
    green pepper--1 large, in chunks
    cold water--2 tablespoons
    cornstarch--1 tablespoon

In a large bowl mix together honey, soy sauce, ketchup and
lemon juice. Place chicken in bowl. Marinate 3 to 4 hours.

Line a shallow baking pan with foil. Dip chicken in marinade. Place skin side up in pan. Pour remaining marinade
over chicken. Bake at 325°F for 1 hour uncovered, basting
occasionally. Add pineapple and green pepper. Bake 15
minutes more. Remove to platter. Mix cornstarch in water.
Stir into gravy to thicken and pour over chicken.

Serves 6.

CHICKEN CACCIATORE

For that special family dinner

chicken fryers--3 lbs., cut up
oil--2 tablespoons
onions--2 medium, diced
garlic--1 clove, crushed
tomatoes--16 oz. can
tomato sauce--8 oz. can
salt--1 teaspoon
oregano--1/2 teaspoon
basil--1/2 teaspoon
celery seed--1/2 teaspoon
bay leaf--2 leaves
white wine--1/4 cup

Brown chicken in oil. Remove. Cook onions in the same pot. Add garlic, tomatoes, tomato sauce, salt, and spices. Mix well. Simmer 3 minutes. Return chicken to pot. Spoon sauce over chicken. Cover. Simmer 30 minutes. Add wine. Cook uncovered an additional 30 minutes. Turn and baste chicken occasionally. Remove bay leaf. Serve with spaghetti using sauce from chicken. Serves 3.

CHICKEN PAPRIKA

An old country favorite

chicken fryer--3 lbs., cut up
flour--3 tablespoons
salt--1 teaspoon
pepper--1/4 teaspoon
chicken fat--2 tablespoons, rendered
onions--1-1/2 cups, chopped
paprika--1 tablespoon
water--1 cup, boiling

Dredge chicken in mixture of flour, salt and pepper. Fry in fat until brown. Remove chicken to 2 quart casserole. Fry onions in pan used to fry chicken using remaining fat. Spread onions over chicken.

Pour water into frying pan. Add paprika. Bring to a boil. Scrape bottom of pan to make a thin gravy. Pour over chicken. Cover. Bake at 350°F for 1 hour or until tender. Chicken may be simmered on top of stove for 1-1/2 hours.

CHICKEN DELIGHTFUL

A quick and easy chicken dish

frying chicken parts--5 to 6 lbs.
onion soup mix--1 to 1-1/2 oz. envelope
Italian salad dressing--16 oz. bottle
oregano--1/2 teaspoon
bay leaves--3 or 4
tomatoes--4 medium, quartered
fresh mushrooms--1/4 lb., sliced
paprika--1/2 teaspoon

add 1/4 cup white wine

Blend onion soup mix, salad dressing, and oregano. Pour
over chicken and marinate for 2 hours. Place chicken in
baking pan with marinade. Top with bay leaves and paprika.
Bake uncovered at 325°F for 60 minutes, basting often, until tender. Add tomatoes and mushrooms. Bake at 325°F for
20 minutes. Good served with noodles.

Serves 8.

MAMA MIA CHICKEN

Easy way of cooking a chicken for your family

chicken fryers--2 (2 to 3 lbs. each)
margarine--6 tablespoons
flour--1/2 cup
salt--2 teaspoons
pepper--1/2 teaspoon
marinara sauce--30 oz.
dried dill weed--2 teaspoons
parsley--2 tablespoons, chopped

Disjoint chicken. Mix flour, salt, and pepper. Dip the
chicken in seasoned flour to coat well. Place in shallow
baking dish one layer deep. Dot with margarine. Bake at
450°F for 25 minutes. Sprinkle with dill weed. Spread
marinara sauce over chicken. Reduce heat to 350°F. Bake
another 25 minutes or until chicken is done. Sprinkle with
parsley. Serves 6 to 8.

Chicken can be frozen before final 25 minutes of baking.

SCAMPI CHICKEN

Excellent

        chicken fryers--2, cut up, or 1 lb. fish
        margarine--1 cup
        sherry wine--1/2 cup
        chopped dill--1 teaspoon, dry
        garlic--2 cloves, crushed
        lemon juice--3 tablespoons
        sugar--2 teaspoons
        Worcestershire sauce--4 teaspoons
        parsley--1/2 cup, minced

Dry chicken or fish with paper towels. Fry in margarine until light brown. Cover and cook on very low heat for 45 minutes, or 7 minutes for fish. Mix wine, dill, garlic, lemon
juice, sugar, and Worcestershire sauce together with margarine remaining in pan. Put chicken in broiler pan and pour
sauce over it. Place under broiler until brown on top.
Cover with parsley and serve.

Serves 4.

HAWAIIAN CHICKEN

Easy and tasty

        chicken fryers--2 (3 lbs. each), or your favorite parts
        oil--3 tablespoons
        onion--1 large, chopped
        ketchup--14 oz.
        water--14 oz.
        white vinegar--2 tablespoons
        brown sugar--1/2 cup
        soy sauce--2 tablespoons
        pineapple chunks--20 oz. can, drained

Saute onion in hot oil until golden brown. Add ketchup,
water, vinegar, and brown sugar. Heat until sugar dissolves. Put chicken in greased casserole and pour sauce
over it. Sprinkle with soy sauce. Bake uncovered at 325°F
for 1 hour and 15 minutes. Baste every 10 minutes. Add
pineapple chunks and bake 15 minutes.

Serves 6.

GLAZED CHICKEN

        chicken parts--3 lbs.
        creamy French dressing--8 oz.
        apricot preserves--8 oz.
        onion soup mix--1 to 1-1/2 oz. envelope

In a bowl large enough to handle chicken pieces, combine
dressing, apricot preserves, and soup mix. Coat chicken
well in mixture and place on a tin foil lined cookie sheet.
Bake uncovered at 325°F for 1-1/2 hours. Serves 4.

OVEN BAKED CHICKEN

                Children's favorite

        frying chicken parts--3 lbs.
        garlic powder--1-1/2 teaspoons
        salt--1/2 teaspoon
        pepper--1/8 teaspoon
        margarine--1/4 cup, melted
        lemon juice--1 tablespoon
        cornflake crumbs--1 cup

Rub chicken with garlic powder, salt, and pepper. Dip
chicken into melted margarine and lemon juice. Roll in the
cornflake crumbs. Coat well. Place in aluminum foil lined
baking dish. Bake covered at 350°F for 30 minutes.
Uncover. Bake 45 minutes until crisp and tender.

Serves 4.

May be frozen before baking.

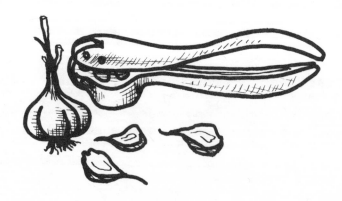

from latkes to lasagna

EGG SALAD MOLD

Even the egg haters love this

        unflavored gelatin--2 envelopes (2 tablespoons)
        cold water--1/2 cup
        boiling water--1 cup
        ketchup--1/2 cup
        mayonnaise--2 cups (1 pint)
        lemon juice--2 tablespoons
        Worcestershire sauce--2 tablespoons
        eggs--18 large, hard cooked
        onion--1 medium, finely chopped

Soften gelatin in cold water. Let stand 5 minutes. Add
boiling water and cool. Add ketchup, mayonnaise, lemon
juice, and Worcestershire sauce. Mix until smooth. Put
eggs through ricer or coarse blade of food grinder. Add
eggs and onion to mayonnaise mixture and mix again.

Pour into a 3 quart buttered ring mold. Chill until firm.
To unmold run a knife around edges of mold and place in
warm water. Quickly turn upside down on a large flat
platter.

Serves 20.

POTATO KUGEL

This is good for Passover as it has no flour

        white potatoes--2-1/2 lbs. (6 medium)
        onion--1 large
        matzo meal--1/2 cup, scant
        salt--1-1/2 teaspoons
        eggs--2 large, beaten
        oil--1/4 cup

Pre-heat oven to 350°F. Peel potatoes, cut into small
pieces, and put through a grinder. Cut onion and put
through grinder. Place this mixture in a bowl and add remaining ingredients. Grease generously a 3 quart casserole.
Pour in batter. Bake at 350°F for 1 hour until golden
brown. Use glass dish in order to watch the browning.

Serves 12.

POTATO LATKES

```
potatoes--4 large, grated
onion--1 medium, grated
egg--1 large
salt--1/2 teaspoon
butter--2 tablespoons, melted
```

Pour the potatoes and onions into a strainer to drain off the excess water. Mix with the other ingredients. Fry in butter over a slow heat. Latkes should cook about 5 minutes on each side.

A blender may be used to grate the potatoes and onions.

OMELETTE

Easy, once you know how

eggs--3 jumbo, strictly fresh
cheddar cheese--1 oz., grated
butter--1 tablespoon

Beat eggs in a copper bowl with a
French whip until egg strings--
about 60 seconds.

Set omelette pan over high heat.
Add butter. Tilt pan back and
forth, covering entire surface with
butter. Turn heat down when butter
bubbles. Add beaten eggs. Pick up
edges slightly with a spatula allowing
uncooked egg on top to run underneath
egg. Work center of egg slightly
with a fork to tell when it begins to
set. At this point cover the egg with
cheese. Carefully fold one half of
egg over the other half with spatula. Continue to fry another 30
seconds. Slide eggs onto a serving dish and eat immediately.

Serves 2.

Try with a variety of fillings such as
fresh mushrooms, peppers, tomatoes,
chopped scallions, or anchovies.

The recipe does not call for salt
but we usually add some
out of force of habit.

120

BAKED YAMS AND APPLES

Don't wait for Thanksgiving to try this

yams--3 lbs. (6 medium), in jackets
apples--4 pippins or Rome Beauty, medium, peeled, and cored
dark brown sugar--1/2 cup
butter--1/4 cup
apple juice--1/2 cup
cornflake crumbs--3 tablespoons
butter--1 tablespoon, softened

Place potatoes in boiling water to cover. Cook 20 minutes.
Peel. Cut into 1/2" thick round slices. Cut apples into
1/4" thick slices. Grease 3 quart pyrex casserole. Place
one slice of potato and one slice of apple next to each
other. Repeat until casserole is filled. Use more than 1
layer, if necessary. Sprinkle with sugar. Dot with 1/4
cup butter. Pour in apple juice. Bake at 350°F for 45
minutes. Mix 1 tablespoon butter with cornflake crumbs.
Sprinkle over top and bake 15 minutes longer.

Serves 12.

BARLEY PILAFF

A nice change from rice

onions--2 medium, chopped
fresh mushrooms--1 cup, chopped
barley--1-1/2 cups
margarine--1/4 cup
pimientos--3, chopped
chicken stock--2 cups
salt--1 teaspoon
pepper--1/8 teaspoon
water--1 cup

Brown onions and mushrooms in margarine. Add barley and
continue to stir until barley is rich tan in color. Put
into casserole, add pimientos, chicken stock, salt and
pepper.

Cover. Bake at 350°F for 30 minutes. Add water and bake
45 minutes more until all liquid is gone and barley is
tender.

121

EGGS CREOLE

A different way to cook eggs

    butter--2 tablespoons
    flour--4 tablespoons
    milk--1 cup
    onions--1/2 cup, diced
    green pepper--1/4 cup, diced
    garlic--1 clove, minced
    tomatoes--16 oz. can, drained
    salt--1/2 teaspoon
    chili powder--1/4 teaspoon
    black olives--6 oz., chopped
    eggs--9 hard cooked, cut in thick slices
    cracker crumbs--1/2 cup
    American cheese--1/2 cup, grated

Melt butter. Stir in flour. Gradually mix in milk. Return to heat and cook until thick. Saute onions, green pepper, and garlic in no stick pan. Grease 1 quart casserole. Layer with eggs. Mix cream sauce, sauteed vegetables, tomatoes, black olives, and seasonings. Pour over eggs. Cover with cracker crumbs and American cheese. Bake at 350°F for 20 minutes or until bubbly.

Serves 5.

RICE CASSEROLE

Easy and pretty enough for company

    instant rice--2 cups
    bouillon--2-1/2 cups
    celery--1 cup, chopped
    carrots--1 cup, grated
    green onions--1/2 cup, chopped
    blanched almonds--1/2 cup, slivered
    parsley--1/2 cup, chopped

Bake rice and bouillon in covered casserole at 350°F for 30 minutes. Add vegetables and nuts to rice. Continue cooking at the same temperature for another 10 minutes.

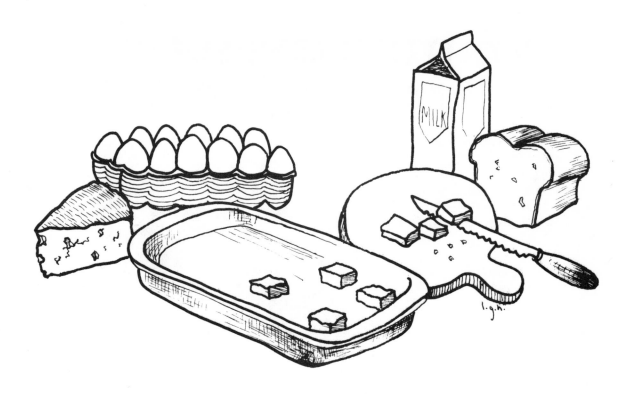

SWISS FONDUE

Eating can be fun

Swiss cheese--1 lb., grated
flour--2 tablespoons
dry white wine or beer--1 cup
nutmeg--1/8 teaspoon
kirsch--2 tablespoons
French bread--1 loaf, cut in 1" squares (some crust on
                                          each square)

Mix cheese with flour until coated. Heat over double boiler. Stir continually. When cheese begins to melt, add
wine (or beer) and blend well. Transfer to heated fondue
dish. Add nutmeg and kirsch. Keep warm.

Give each guest a large fondue fork and a handful of bread
pieces so he can dip bread in hot cheese. If he drops the
bread off the fork into the cheese, he must kiss all guests
of the opposite sex.

POTATO CHEESE PUDDING

Not like mother used to make

potato pancake mix--2 pkgs. (6 oz. each)
oil--1/2 cup
baking powder--2 teaspoons
eggs--4 large
water--2-1/2 cups
cheddar cheese--1/4 lb., grated

Mix ingredients together well. Add more water if mixture is thicker than cake batter. Pour into 9" casserole. Bake at 350°F for 40 minutes.

CHEESE KNAIDLACH

A family favorite

hoop cheese--1 lb.
egg--1 large
flour--2 tablespoons
salt--1/8 teaspoon
pepper--1/8 teaspoon
sugar--1 teaspoon
butter--2 tablespoons, melted
graham crackers--2, crumbled fine

Set aside butter and cracker crumbs. Mix all other ingredients together. Blend well. With damp hands roll into small balls. Drop balls into boiling water. Bring water back to a full boil, and boil about 1 minute. Remove with slotted spoon and drop into dish of melted butter. Then coat balls with graham cracker crumbs and serve warm with sour cream.

A different kind of dessert. These may be frozen before cooking. Place on a cookie sheet. Cover well. Freeze.

Serves 4 to 5.

CHEESE BLINTZES

Crepes:

eggs--2 large
water--1-1/2 cups
flour--1 cup
salt--1 teaspoon

Beat eggs slightly. Add water, salt, and flour. Beat until smooth. A few lumps will not matter.

Heat a heavy skillet. Brush with a solid shortening. Drop a large spoonful of batter into the frying pan. Tilt pan in all directions so that batter covers entire surface. Put pan down on a medium flame. When the edges of the crepe begin to curl up slightly and there are no uncooked areas on the surface, turn the crepe onto a large piece of wax paper by inverting the frying pan and tapping it slightly on one edge. If crepe does not fall free, loosen it with a spatula.

Grease pan with a brush after each crepe. If crepes continue to stick to pan after a few are made, stop and scour the pan and start over. Crepes may be stacked as they are cooked. Keep covered with a towel until used.

Filling:

hoop cheese--1 lb.
lemon juice--1/2 teaspoon
sugar--1 teaspoon
butter--2 tablespoons
vanilla--1/4 teaspoon
eggs--2 large, slightly beaten

Mix all ingredients for filling. Place 2 tablespoons of filling in center of each blintz skin or crepe. Fold bottom half over cheese, then the two sides and lastly fold the top over the center. Place each filled blintz fold down in a pan with melted butter. Fry slowly 7 minutes on each side, or place filled blintzes in a baking dish. Dot with butter. Bake at 350°F for 1 hour. Serve with cinnamon and sugar or sour cream.

Blintzes are often filled with apple sauce, blueberries, or other berries.

****

"My spikenard sent forth its fragrance." (Song of Songs)

RICE ALA POLONAISE

        rice--1 cup, regular
        margarine--4 tablespoons
        water--1 cup
        beef broth--1 can (10-1/2 oz.)
        onions--2 tablespoons, instant dried

Mix all ingredients together. Bring to a boil. Cover,
lower, and simmer until all liquid is absorbed. Mix again
and serve.

Serves 5.

QUICK QUICHE

        It was my turn to bring the main dish
        And I thought that this was delish--
                But my dear family spied it
                And of course tried it
        And the pot that I brought held gornisht!

    white bread--16 slices, crusts removed
    processed American cheese--6 oz., frozen for easy grating
    eggs--6 large
    milk--2 cups
    salt--1/4 teaspoon
    butter--1/4 cup, melted

Butter a 9" x 15" casserole. Line with one layer of bread.
Grate half of cheese over bread. Layer on the rest of the
bread. Grate the remainder of the cheese over bread.

Beat eggs and milk together until foamy. Add salt. Pour
over bread and cheese in casserole. Pour butter evenly
over top.

Cover with foil and refrigerate overnight. Remove from refrigerator 1-1/2 hours before baking.

Place casserole in a pan of water. Bake at 400°F for 1
hour or until nice and brown on top. Serves 10.

Recipe can be divided into 24 foil muffin tins. Bake as
above and serve as hors d'oeuvres. Your guests will love
these.

CHILI RELLENO PIE

If I bake this once more, my family
  will be speaking fluent Spanish

green chilies--4 cans (4 oz. each)
jack cheese--1 lb., sliced
cheddar cheese--1 lb., sliced
flour--4 tablespoons
evaporated milk--2 cups
eggs--4 large
tomato sauce--2 cups

Cut chilies open and remove center vein. Line a 9" x 12"
baking dish with the chilies. Layer both the pie jack cheese
and the cheddar cheese evenly over the chilies. Add the
rest of the chilies over the cheese.

Mix the flour carefully with a small amount of the milk to
make a smooth paste. Mix in the rest of the milk, beat in
the eggs, and pour over the chilies and cheese.

Bake for 30 minutes at 350°F. Add tomato sauce over top
and bake for another 15 minutes. Nice with a green salad.

Serves 12.

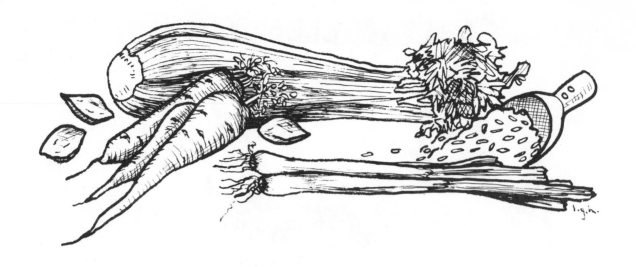

CONFETTI RICE

Party rice

        rice--1 cup (not instant)
        water--1-1/2 cups
        salt--1 teaspoon
        butter--1/2 cup
        eggs--2 large, slightly beaten
        bean sprouts--16 oz. can
        green onions--1 cup, chopped, tops and bottoms
        pimiento strips--1/2 cup chopped

Add rice to boiling, salted water. Lower heat. Cook until
all liquid is absorbed. Set aside but do not let rice cool.
In a large frying pan or electric skillet melt butter. Add
eggs, stirring continuously until eggs are slightly cooked.
Remove from heat. Add rice. Add all other ingredients. Mix
well and heat. Prepare recipe, all at once, and do not
double or freeze.

Serves 10.

ITALIAN MACARONI AND CHEESE

Lasagne's Second Cousin

        oil--4 tablespoons
        onion--1/2 cup, chopped
        celery--1/4 cup, chopped
        garlic--1 clove, minced
        tomato paste--6 oz. can
        water--2-1/2 cups
        salt--1 teaspoon
        pepper--1/8 teaspoon
        oregano--1/4 teaspoon
        basil--1/4 teaspoon
        sugar--1/4 teaspoon
        Parmesan cheese--1/2 cup, grated
        macaroni--8 oz., cooked and drained
        Ricotta or cottage cheese--1 lb. (2 cups)

Saute onion, celery, and garlic in oil until soft. Add
tomato paste, water, seasonings, and sugar. Bring to a
boil and then lower heat. Simmer 1 hour. Put thin layer
of sauce in a 9" x 9" baking dish. Sprinkle with 2 tablespoons of Parmesan cheese. Top with half of macaroni and
add Ricotta or cottage cheese. Cover with half of the remaining sauce and sprinkle with 3 tablespoons of Parmesan
cheese. Add the rest of macaroni and sauce. Sprinkle top
with 3 tablespoons of Parmesan cheese. Bake at 350°F for
30 minutes. Freezes well. Serves 6.

POPPY SEED NOODLES

Good with brisket and gravy

        broad egg noodles--8 oz., cooked as directed on box
        butter--1/4 cup, melted
        poppy seeds--1 tablespoon
        slivered almonds--1/2 cup, toasted
        fresh lemon juice--1 tablespoon
        salt--1/4 teaspoon

Add poppy seeds, almonds, lemon juice, and salt to melted
butter. Pour over hot noodles and toss lightly with fork.

Serves 6.

KUGEL QUARTET

The best of four recipes

wide noodles--8 oz., cooked as directed on box
eggs--3 large
milk--3/4 cup
sour cream--3/4 cup
butter--1/4 cup, soft
sugar--1/2 cup
LG CURD COTTAGE CHEESE & 4oz CREAM CHEESE

Beat egg slightly. Mix egg, milk, sour cream, butter, and
sugar in a large bowl. Fold in noodles. Pour into well
buttered 8" x 8" baking dish. Bake at 325°F for 1-1/2
hours. Cut into 2" squares. Good hot or cold.

Variations:

Topping:

cornflakes--1 cup, crushed
butter--2 tablespoons, melted
sugar--2 tablespoons
cinnamon--1/2 teaspoon
Mix and crumble over kugel before baking.

Additions to filling:

white raisins--1/4 cup
cinnamon--1/2 teaspoon
Add to noodles before baking.

crushed pineapple--8 oz. can
maraschino cherries--3 oz. jar
Add to noodles before baking.

cheddar cheese--1 cup, grated
Add to noodles before baking. Omit sugar in filling.
Do not use with sweet topping.

Serves 8.

****

*"They should be fed with the fat of wheat; and with honey
out of the rock would I satisfy them." (Psalms)*

CAPTAIN'S KUGEL

This dish can be mixed one day ahead

     wide egg noodles--1 lb.
     boiling water--6 quarts
     salt--3-1/2 teaspoons
     sugar--4 tablespoons
     sour cream--1 pint
     milk--1 cup
     large curd cottage cheese--1 lb.
     butter--6 tablespoons, melted
     cornflakes--1 cup, crushed
     butter--2 tablespoons, broken in bits

Cook noodles in boiling water and 1 teaspoon salt. Remove
when tender. Do not overcook. Mix sour cream, cottage
cheese, milk, 2-1/2 teaspoons salt, sugar, and melted butter together. Mix with noodles and pour into 3 quart casserole. Cover with cornflakes and bits of butter. Bake at
375°F for 1-1/2 hours. This pudding never sets firm enough
to cut. Serve hot. Serves 12.

ENVIOUS GREEN LASAGNE

Your friends will wish they had this recipe

```
lasagne noodles--8 oz., cooked as directed on package
onions--1 medium, chopped
olive oil--1 tablespoon
fresh mushrooms--1/2 lb., chopped
tomato paste--6 oz. can
water--12 oz.
salt--1-1/2 teaspoons
sugar--1 teaspoon
basil--1/2 teaspoon
pepper--1/8 teaspoon
oregano--1 teaspoon
Mozzarella cheese--1 lb., sliced
frozen chopped spinach--10 oz. pkg., thawed and drained
Ricotta cheese--1 lb., soft
Parmesan cheese--1/2 cup, grated
```

Saute onions in olive oil until transparent. Add mushrooms and
saute slowly for 5 minutes. Add tomato paste, water, salt,
sugar, and spices. Simmer for 1 hour.

Butter well a 9" x 15" baking dish.

In the following order layer the pan:

```
1/3 of sauce
1/3 of the noodles
all of the Mozzarella cheese
1/2 of the spinach
1/3 of the noodles
1/3 of the sauce
all of the Ricotta cheese crumbled
1/2 of the spinach
1/3 of the noodles
1/3 of the sauce
all of the Parmesan cheese sprinkled over top.
```

Bake at 350°F for 1 hour. Cut into squares. Serve with
Italian salad. Serves 10.

"That thou mayest give them their food in due season."
(Psalms)

QUICHE LORRAINE

We used this for a 25th anniversary party

pastry dough for a 10" shell--you may use a ready made shell
onion--1 large, sliced and sauteed
eggs--3 large
milk--1-1/2 cups
nutmeg--1/4 teaspoon
salt--1/2 teaspoon
pepper--1/16 teaspoon
Swiss cheese--1 cup, grated

Roll dough into a circle to fit a flan dish or 9" pie plate.
Press dough gently into pan. Cut the excess dough leaving
the sides even with the rim. Prick bottom of dough with
fork extremely well. Bake at 450°F until lightly browned.

Line shell with the sauteed onions. Blend eggs, milk, seasonings, and cheese very well. Pour over onions. Bake at
375°F for about 30 minutes or until knife comes clean from
center.

Serves 4 as a main course or 8 for hors d'oeuvres.

HELPFUL HINTS

Always have ingredients at room temperature.

Measure flour after sifting.

When using nuts, dust with flour so nuts will remain separate.

When using melted chocolate, always cool before adding to butter.

When recipe calls for egg yolks only, save whites in covered jar
in refrigerator. May be kept for eight weeks.

To make smooth cream sauces, warm milk before adding.

To tint coconut, toss in a bowl with a few drops of food coloring.
Blot with a towel.

For an extra kick when serving fruit juice, add a little ginger ale
or sherbet.

from brioche to bagels

FRIDAY NIGHT CHALLAH

Looks like a picture

    dry yeast--1 pkg.
    water--1 cup
    sugar--2 tablespoons
    salt--1 teaspoon
    eggs--2 large
    oil--2 tablespoons
    flour--2 to 3-1/2 cups
    egg yolk--1 large
    poppy or sesame seeds (optional)

Pour lukewarm water into a large mixing bowl. Sprinkle in yeast and stir until thoroughly dissolved. Add sugar and salt and stir well. Add eggs and beat with beater. Add oil and beat slightly. Gradually stir in 3 cups of flour, mix well. Place dough on floured board and knead 3 to 4 minutes. Add more flour while kneading, if necessary. Dough should feel smooth and elastic, not sticky. Place dough in slightly oiled large bowl. Brush top of dough with oil and cover bowl with warm wet cloth.

Let dough rise until tripled in size (about 2 to 3 hours). Dough will rise more quickly if bowl is placed in a warm spot. Be sure bowl is not near an open window or in a draft.

After dough rises, remove to floured board and pound out air with fists. Divide dough into 4 equal parts. Stretch and roll 3 of them until about 1-1/2" thick. Twist the 3 parts into a braid. Place on greased cookie sheet. Divide the remaining quarter into 3 parts and stretch and roll each part about 1/2" thick. Twist into braid and place on the larger braid. Brush with beaten egg yolk. Sprinkle with poppy or sesame seeds. Let rise 10 to 15 minutes.

Bake in pre-heated oven at 350°F for 1 hour. To prove this was really an easy Challah to make, I had my son make this, and it came out looking like a picture.

Makes a 1-1/2 lb. loaf.

"'Make ready quickly three measures of fine meal, knead it and make cakes.' and Abraham ran unto the herd and fetched a calf tender and good". (Genesis)

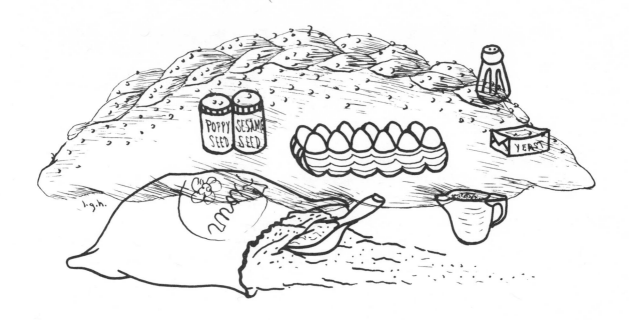

BAVARIAN PANCAKES

These are tender and delicious

    eggs--3 large
    milk--3/4 cup
    flour--3/4 cup
    nutmeg--1/16 teaspoon
    butter--6 tablespoons, soft
    powdered sugar--6 tablespoons, sifted
    lemon--1/2 medium (use juice only)

Pre-heat oven to 450°F.

Beat eggs, milk, and flour together to make a smooth paste.
Add nutmeg. Spread butter over bottom of two 9" cake or
pie tins. Pour 1/2 of batter evenly in each tin. Bake for
10 minutes. Pancake will cook with an irregular surface.
Remove from oven. Sprinkle sugar over each pancake. Place
back in oven for 3 minutes. Remove from oven. Squeeze a
little lemon juice over each pancake. Slip onto a heated
plate.

Serves 2.

137

MONKEY BREAD

Even better than your cateress makes!

    milk--2 cups
    butter--1 cup, softened
    sugar--1/2 cup
    salt--1-1/2 teaspoons
    dry yeast--2 pkgs., dissolved in 1/2 cup lukewarm water
    eggs--2 large
    flour--6 cups
    butter--1 cup melted

Scald milk and allow to cool. Add softened butter, sugar,
and salt to milk. Add the yeast and eggs when milk feels a
bit too cool for a baby's bath. Mix well. Allow to stand
at room temperature until yeast forms a froth on top of the
milk.

Measure flour into a large bowl. Make well in center of
flour. Pour in milk and yeast solution. Mix well. Knead
for about 10 minutes. Cover tightly and allow to sit in
warm place for about 1 hour until triple in volume. Punch
down with your hand and allow to rise again.

Form bread by tearing off 3" pieces of the dough. Dip in
the melted butter. Place buttered pieces in a 6 cup ring
mold. Continue until mold is 3/4 full. Allow to set again
until they increase about 25% in size. Bake at 350°F for
about 45 minutes. Allow to cool 10 minutes. Unmold onto
serving plate.

Serves 12.

OVERNIGHTERS

The best rolls I ever tasted

        dry yeast--1 pkg.
        milk--1 cup
        butter--3/4 cup, melted
        salt--1/2 teaspoon
        sugar--1/4 cup
        eggs--2 large, slightly beaten
        flour--4 cups

Dissolve yeast in slightly warm milk. Allow to stand until yeast forms a froth over top of milk. Add butter, salt, sugar, and eggs. Mix.

Make well in center of flour. Pour in other ingredients and mix well. Knead for about 2 minutes. Cover tightly and store in refrigerator overnight. Dough will double in size by morning. Remove from refrigerator 2-1/2 hours before baking. Divide dough into 4 parts. Roll each section into a circle 1/2" thick.

Cut into 12 pie-shaped pieces. Roll each piece from the big end to small point. Put rolls on ungreased sheet. Let rise in a warm place for about 2 hours or until twice as large.

Bake at 350°F for 10 to 15 minutes. Watch carefully and remove from oven when lightly browned. Makes 48.

BRIOCHE

        overnighters dough--1 recipe
        milk--1 tablespoon

Set aside 1/4 of dough.

Divide remaining dough into 24 paper cake cups. Set each cup in a cup cake pan. Press a hole in the middle of each roll with your finger.

Form 24 balls from the remaining dough. Place one ball over each depression in larger roll. Brush with milk. Bake in 350°F oven for 15 to 20 minutes.

Serve with home-made jam.

GARLIC CHEESE BREAD

A favorite with children and grown-ups

flour--2-1/4 cups, sifted
salt--1 teaspoon
Italian mixed herbs--1-1/4 teaspoons
baking powder--1-1/2 teaspoons
baking soda--1/2 teaspoon
garlic powder--1/4 teaspoon
butter--1/3 cup, softened
eggs--2 large, beaten
sour cream--1/2 pint (1 cup)
sharp cheddar cheese--2 cups, shredded

Sift flour, salt, baking powder, baking soda, and garlic powder in a bowl. Add mixed herbs. Cut in softened butter with a pastry blender or two knives. Add eggs and sour cream.

Mix well. Blend in cheese and mix again. Turn into two 4" x 9" greased and floured pans.

Bake at 350°F for 55 to 60 minutes. Cool in pan 10 minutes and turn out.

When cool, slice thin. Freeze or refrigerate in tinfoil.

PUMPKIN BREAD

Surprise your friends with something different

        oil--8 oz.
        sugar--3 cups
        eggs--4 large
        flour--3-1/3 cups, sifted
        baking soda--2 teaspoons
        cinnamon--1 teaspoon
        nutmeg--1 teaspoon
        cloves--1 teaspoon
        salt--1/2 teaspoon
        pumpkin--16 oz. can
        water--2/3 cup
        butter--1/2 cup

Combine oil and sugar. Mix well. Add eggs, 1 at a time, and mix again. Sift flour with baking soda, cinnamon, nutmeg, cloves, and salt. Mix pumpkin with water. Add dry ingredients to batter, alternately with pumpkin mixture.

Pour into 3 well greased loaf pans, 4" x 9". Bake at 350°F for 1 hour. Cool. Remove from pans. Slice, butter, and wrap in tin foil. Re-heat in tin foil. These may be frozen.

Each loaf serves 10.

QUICK GARLIC BREAD

Another favorite

    sour dough French rolls--6 medium (or regular)
    butter--1/2 cup, softened
    garlic--1 clove, crushed
    cheddar or American cheese--4 oz., shredded

Pre-heat oven to 350°F.

Slice rolls in half, the long way.

Mix garlic and butter. Spread on rolls. Sprinkle with cheese and place on a cookie sheet.

Bake for 5 minutes until cheese is melted; or prepare and cover with tin foil, freeze, and bake later.

PASSOVER PUFFS

Ours disappeared before they were even filled

        shortening--1/4 cup
        sugar--2 teaspoons
        salt--1/2 teaspoon
        boiling water--1 cup
        matzo cake meal--1 cup
        eggs--3 large

Add shortening, sugar, and salt to boiling water. Stir in cake meal when fat has melted. Stir rapidly until well blended. Remove from heat and cool slightly. Beat in eggs, one at a time, until dough is smooth. Drop from tablespoon onto well greased cookie sheet. Bake at 325°F for 40 minutes. Fill with gefilte fish, chicken salad, or tuna.

PASSOVER BAGEL

My guests took home all that were left over

        water--2/3 cup
        fat--1/3 cup
        sugar--1 tablespoon
        salt--1/4 teaspoon
        matzo meal--1 cup
        eggs--3 large

Mix water, fat, sugar, and salt in pot. Bring to a boil. Remove from flame. Add matzo meal. Continue to boil until thick and immediately remove from heat. When cool, add eggs 1 at a time and beat well with a fork. Place on sheet about 1" apart. Dip wet finger in the center of each ball to make the hole. Bake at 375°F for about 3/4 hour. These will puff up and turn golden brown and may be kept for about 2 days. Makes about 3 dozen.

****

"Go thy way, eat thy bread with joy, and drink with a merry heart." (Ecclesiastes)

QUICK APPLE BREAD

A light dessert

        flour--2 cups, sifted
        baking powder--1 teaspoon
        baking soda--1 teaspoon
        sugar--1 cup
        butter-1/2 cup
        eggs--2 large
        buttermilk--4 tablespoons
        apples--1 cup, unpeeled, minced
        chopped walnuts--1/4 cup
        vanilla--1 teaspoon

Sift flour, baking powder, and baking soda together.

Cream sugar and butter
until creamy. Beat in
eggs one at a time.

Add flour, alternating
with the milk.

Then add apples,
nuts, and vanilla.
Mix well.

Pour into well
buttered
8" x 10"
bread pan.

Bake at 350°F
for 1 hour

Serves 8.

WHOLE WHEAT BREAD

Fortified and delicious

dry yeast--1 pkg.
water--1 cup, lukewarm
sugar--1 tablespoon
whole wheat flour--5 cups
wheat germ--5 cups
salt--1 tablespoon
anise--1 tablespoon
milk--2 cups
eggs--4 large
margarine--1 cup, soft
molasses--1 cup
cream--2 tablespoons

Mix the yeast with 1 cup lukewarm water. Add sugar. Allow yeast to stand until a froth forms on top of sugar solution. Place dry ingredients in a bowl. Mix in milk, dissolved yeast, and margarine. Then add eggs. Beat on slow speed for about 5 minutes. Cover tightly with plastic. Allow to sit in warm spot. Dough should rise in about 2 hours. When it has doubled its size, punch down and allow to double again. Now divide dough into 2 pieces. Place in 2 well buttered 4" x 9" bread pans. Pan must have sides as dough is soft. Brush top with cream. Bake at 350°F for 45 minutes. Test with a toothpick. When it comes clean, bread is done.

Remove from pan immediately and wrap in clean cloth dish towel.

One slice of this bread gives you about 15% of your iron, 30% of your vitamin E, and about 25% of your protein requirements for the day--plus 200 calories!

HELPFUL HINTS

For attractive salads, dip lettuce leaf edge in paprika.

Julienne salami adds a gourmet touch to everyday salads.

When recipe calls for white sauce, try using a canned cream soup.

When pan frying potatoes, use 1/3 olive oil and 2/3 cooking oil. This lends an exotic flavor.

from Kuchen to cakes

MULTI-DELICIOUS CAKE

If you saw this at the bakery, you'd buy it

       cocoa--1/2 cup, sifted
       water--1 cup, boiling
       cake flour--1-3/8 cup, sifted
       baking powder--1/4 teaspoon
       baking soda--1 teaspoon
       salt--1/4 teaspoon
       butter--1/2 cup
       sugar--1-1/4 cups
       eggs--2 large
       vanilla--1 teaspoon

Pre-heat oven to 350°F. Grease 10" x 10" cake pan. Line bottom with wax paper.

Combine cocoa and water. Beat until smooth. Sift dry ingredients. Beat softened butter, sugar and eggs together until very light and fluffy. Alternately add cooled cocoa and flour to egg mixture. Do not overbeat. Pour into tin and bake 25 to 30 minutes at 350°F. Remove from oven when center of cake springs back slightly to touch. Let stand 5 minutes and remove from pan and place on cooling rack. Slice through center making 2 layers.

Filling:

butter--1/2 cup
sugar--1/2 cup
flour--2-1/2 tablespoons
milk--1/2 cup
vanilla--1/2 teaspoon
chopped pecans--1/2 cup

Beat butter and sugar together until very fluffy--about 5 minutes. Mix flour and milk together in a small pot. Cook until thick, stirring constantly. Cool. Add a small amount of sugar mixture to flour paste to thin. Carefully mix the remainder of sugar mixture with flour paste. Add nuts and vanilla. Spread filling between split layers. Place the other half back on the first half.

MULTI-DELICIOUS FROSTING

For the Multi-Delicious Chocolate Cake

semi-sweet chocolate--6 oz.
milk--1/4 cup
butter--1/2 cup
powdered sugar--1-1/4 cups

Melt chocolate with milk and butter. Stir with fork until
smooth. Remove from heat. Beat in the sugar. Place bowl
over ice (or use a mixing bowl which has been placed in
freezer). Continue to beat until thick enough to spread.
Ice cake immediately because frosting tends to thicken as
it sets.

CHOCOLATE CHIP CAKE

dark chocolate cake mix--18 oz.
sour cream--1/2 pint (1 cup)
warm water--1/4 cup
chocolate instant pudding--3-3/4 oz. pkg.
oil--1/4 cup
eggs--4 large
semi-sweet chocolate chips--6 oz.

Mix all ingredients except chocolate chips at low speed until well moistened. Increase to medium speed and beat 3 minutes. Fold in chocolate chips. Bake in well greased angel
food cake pan at 350°F for 50 minutes or in a well greased
oblong glass pan at 325°F for 50 minutes or until tooth pick
comes out clean. Serves 10.

CHOCOLATE MOCHA CAKE

devil's food or fudge cake mix--18 oz. pkg.
strong coffee--1-1/2 cups
eggs--2 large

Mix cake mix, coffee, and eggs at low speed until well
moistened. Beat for 2 minutes at medium speed. Bake in
two 9" round, well greased pans at 350°F for 25 minutes.

Ice with fluffy chocolate frosting.

LEMON SURPRISE CAKE

LEMON SURPRISE CAKE

      white or yellow cake mix--18 oz. pkg.
      instant lemon pudding--3 oz. box
      cold water--1 cup
      eggs--4 large
      nuts--1/2 cup, finely ground
      powdered sugar--2 tablespoons for garnish

Put all ingredients except powdered sugar in mixing bowl.
Blend slowly until well moistened. Beat at high speed for
3 minutes. Pour into well greased 10" angel food cake pan.
Bake at 350°F for 50 to 55 minutes. Cake is done when it
springs back when you touch it with your finger. Cool and
remove from pan. Dust with powdered sugar. Serves 10.

FRUIT CHEESE CAKE

Easy and perfect every time

      graham crackers--1-1/2 cups (22), crumbled
      butter--1/2 cup, melted
      vanilla--1 tablespoon
      lemon juice--4 tablespoons
      sweetened condensed milk--14 oz. can
      cream cheese--8 oz., softened
      fruit pie filling--21 oz. can (your favorite)

Combine crumbs and butter and press into a 9" pie plate. Bake at 350°F for 5 minutes. Cool. Gradually add vanilla, lemon juice, and condensed milk to the softened cream cheese. Mix until well blended. Pour into shell and refrigerate. When cheese is firm, about 1 hour later, pour pie filling over. Refrigerate until serving time.

Serves 8.

CHEDDAR CHEESE CAKE

I wish my mother had made cheese cake like this

Crust:

flour--1 cup
sugar--1/4 cup
butter--1/2 cup
egg yolk--1
lemon rind--1 teaspoon, grated
vanilla--1/4 teaspoon

Filling:

cream cheese--32 oz.
cheddar cheese--1 cup, grated
imitation vanilla--1/4 teaspoon
lemon rind--1/2 teaspoon, grated
orange rind--1/2 teaspoon, grated
eggs--4 whole eggs plus 2 yolks
sugar--1-3/4 cup
beer--1/4 cup
whipping cream--1/4 cup

Mix ingredients for crust. Press 1/3 of dough into bottom of spring form. This is a big cake. Bake at 400°F for 10 minutes. Remove from oven and press in the rest of dough around edges of pan to within 1" of top of pan.

Mix cheeses and flavorings together. Add the whole eggs, 1 at a time, beating well after each addition. Add yolks and sugar. Beat well.

Stir in the beer and cream carefully. Pour into crust. Bake at 500°F for 8 minutes and then reduce heat to 250°F and bake for another 1-1/2 hours. Turn off oven, but leave cake in closed oven for at least 1 hour. Serves at least 12.

ICE BOX CAKE

        strawberry gelatin--3 oz. pkg.
        boiling water--3/4 cup
        cold water--1/2 cup
        marble cake mix--18 oz. pkg.
        imitation whipped cream topping--1 oz. pkg.
        instant vanilla pudding--3 oz. pkg.
        milk--1-1/2 cups, cold
        vanilla--1 teaspoon
        strawberries--1 box, stems removed

Dissolve gelatin in boiling water. Add cold water. Set
aside at room temperature. Prepare cake mix and bake according to directions. Use a 13" x 9" cake pan. Cool cake
20 minutes. Using a fork, poke holes in cake about 1"
apart. Slowly pour gelatin mixture into the holes. Refrigerate cake. Slice half of the berries. In a chilled bowl
blend topping mix, instant pudding, milk, and vanilla. Whip
until stiff, about 5 minutes.

Remove cake from refrigerator. Top with sliced berries.
Frost with whipped mixture. Garnish with whole berries.
Refrigerate until served. Serves 16.

CHOCOLATE FUDGE CAKE

                A rich, fine textured cake

        butter--1/2 cup
        sugar--1 cup
        vanilla--1 teaspoon
        eggs--4 large
        chocolate syrup--16 oz. can
        flour--1 cup, sifted
        baking powder--1 teaspoon

Cream butter and sugar. Add vanilla, eggs, and syrup. Mix
thoroughly.

Sift flour and baking powder together. Blend into batter.

Pour into a well buttered 9" x 9" pan. Bake at 325°F for 1
hour or until done. If you use a tube pan, double the
recipe. The cake may be sprinkled with powdered sugar if
desired. Serves 8.

A CLOUD OF A CAKE

Light, fluffy, and so delicious

        graham crackers--2 squares, crumbled fine
        eggs--10 large (5 whole, 5 separated)
        sugar--2 cups
        cream cheese--2-1/4 lbs., softened
        sour cream--1-1/2 pints (3 cups)
        vanilla--1 teaspoon
        lemon juice--2 tablespoons
        cake flour--5 tablespoons, sifted

Pre-heat oven to 300°F. Butter spring form. Shake half the
cracker crumbs evenly over tin.

Combine 5 yolks with 5 whole eggs. Beat until very creamy,
about 5 minutes. Set aside.

Beat 5 whites to soft peaks and set aside.

Cream sugar and cream cheese together. Add sour cream, vanilla, and lemon juice. Add flour. Mix well.

Fold the egg yolk mixture into the cream cheese.

Very carefully fold in the beaten egg whites.

Pour batter into pan and cover with remaining cracker
crumbs. Bake 1 hour and 20 minutes or until firm in middle.
Turn off heat and leave cake in oven with door open for 1
hour. May be served warm. Serves 12.

NO BAKE FRUITCAKE

For the liberated woman

evaporated milk--1/2 cup
marshmallows--16, cut fine
orange juice--3 tablespoons
graham crackers--4 dozen, rolled fine
cinnamon--1/4 teaspoon
nutmeg--1/4 teaspoon
cloves--1/8 teaspoon
pitted dates--1/2 cup, cut fine
raisins--1 cup (dark and light mixed)
chopped walnuts--1-1/2 cups
mixed candied fruit--2 cups
candied orange peel--2 tablespoons

Put milk, marshmallows, and orange juice in a bowl for 5
minutes. Mix graham crackers, spices, dried fruits, and
nuts. Add mixture of milk, marshmallows, and orange juice.
Continue mixing with your impeccably clean hands.

Line 5 cup loaf pan with waxed paper. Press cake firmly into pan. Decorate as desired with nuts and fruits. Cover
tightly. Chill in refrigerator at least 2 days before
slicing. Makes a 2-1/4 lb. cake.

BANANA NUT CAKE

Something for everyone

sugar--2 cups
butter--1/2 cup, softened
eggs--2 large
banana--1 medium, mashed
vanilla--1 teaspoon
sour cream--1 pint (2 cups)
flour--3 cups, sifted
baking powder--2 teaspoons
baking soda--2 teaspoons
salt--1 teaspoon

brown sugar--1/3 cup
cinnamon--2 teaspoons
chopped nuts--1 cup
semi-sweet chocolate chips--6 oz.

Blend sugar, butter, and eggs. Add banana, vanilla, and sour cream. Mix well.

Sift dry ingredients. Add to batter and blend thoroughly. Pour half into a well greased 9" x 12" baking pan.

Mix brown sugar, cinnamon, and chopped nuts with chocolate chips. Spread half of this over batter. Add the rest of batter. Cover with remaining sugar and nuts. Bake at 350°F for 45 minutes. Serves 12.

FILLED CHOCOLATE CAKE

A most unusual dessert

flour--1-1/2 cups, sifted
sugar--1 cup
baking soda--1 teaspoon
salt--1/2 teaspoon
cocoa--1/4 cup
egg--1 large
white vinegar--1 tablespoon
oil--1/3 cup
vanilla--1 teaspoon

Topping:

cream cheese--8 oz.
egg--1 large
sugar--1/3 cup
salt--1/8 teaspoon
semi-sweet chocolate chips--6 oz.

Sift flour, sugar, soda, and 1/2 teaspoon salt together. Add cocoa. Blend well to work lumps out of cocoa. Put 1 egg in bottom of a measuring cup. Add water to make 1 cup. Combine with vinegar, oil, and vanilla. Mix into dry ingredients.

Place 20 foil cups in muffin tins. Half fill each one with this batter.

Blend cream cheese, 1 egg, 1/3 cup sugar, and 1/8 teaspoon salt. Add the chocolate chips. Spoon over batter.

Bake at 350°F for 30 minutes.

TOMATO SOUP CAKE

Add a little spice to your life

sugar--1 cup
shortening--1/2 cup
tomato soup--10-1/2 oz. can
baking soda--1 teaspoon, dissolved in soup
flour--2 cups
baking powder--2 teaspoons
salt--1/8 teaspoon
cinnamon--1 teaspoon
cloves--1/2 teaspoon
nutmeg--1/2 teaspoon
chopped nuts--1 cup
seedless raisins--1-1/2 cups

Use an electric mixer. Blend all ingredients together except nuts and raisins. Fold in nuts and raisins by hand.

When well mixed, pour into a glass loaf pan 5" x 9" lined with wax paper on bottom.

Bake at 350°F for 30 to 40 minutes.

CHERRY DUMP COBBLER

A fast and easy dessert

cherry pie filling--21 oz. can
lemon juice--1 tablespoon
crushed pineapple--16 oz. can, undrained
white or yellow cake mix--18 oz. pkg.
butter--3/4 cup
chopped walnuts--1/2 cup

Pour cherry pie filling and lemon juice into a greased 9" x 14" cake pan. Pour pineapple on top of cherry mixture. Sprinkle dry cake mix on top of pineapple and crumble butter on top. Sprinkle with nuts. Bake at 350°F for 1 hour. Good served warm with either whipped cream or vanilla ice cream.

Serves 8 to 10.

154

STRUDEL CAKE

Good to look at and good to eat

```
flour--3-1/2 cups, sifted
baking powder--1 tablespoon
salt--1/2 teaspoon
butter--1/2 cup, softened
eggs--3 large, beaten
vanilla--1/2 teaspoon
sugar--1-1/2 cups
orange juice--1/2 cup

crushed pineapple--16 oz. can, well drained
raisins--1/2 box (7-1/2 oz.)
cracker crumbs--1/2 cup
chopped nuts--3/4 cup
cinnamon--1 teaspoon
strawberry jam--10 oz. (or your favorite)
```

Sift flour with baking powder and salt. Make well in middle
of flour. Add butter, eggs, vanilla, 1/2 cup of sugar, and
orange juice into well. Mix ingredients in well with a fork,
gradually incorporating flour to make a soft dough. Divide
into 3 parts. Roll 1/3 of dough to fit a 13" x 15" pan.
Put dough into unbuttered pan.

Mix pineapple, raisins, crumbs, nuts, 1/2 cup of sugar, and
cinnamon together. Spread half of this filling over first
layer of dough. Dribble half of jam over filling. Roll out
next layer and repeat. Cover with third layer. Sprinkle
1/2 cup of sugar on top. Bake at 350°F for 50 minutes.
Cool. Cut into squares. Freeze and use as needed.

VANISHING CAKE

It disappears quickly

        dates--1 cup, chopped
        water--1-1/2 cups, boiling
        baking soda--2-1/4 teaspoons
        butter--3/4 cup
        sugar--1-1/3 cups
        eggs--2 large
        cake flour--1-3/4 cup, sifted
        chopped walnuts or pecans--3/4 cup
        semi-sweet chocolate chips--6 oz.

Put dates, boiling water, and 1-1/2 teaspoons soda into blender. If you do not have a blender, chop dates well. Cream butter and 1 cup sugar. Add eggs, 1 at a time, beating after each addition. Sift 3/4 teaspoon soda and flour together. Add dry ingredients to egg mixture, alternating with dates. Fold together carefully.

Butter a 9" x 12" pan. Line bottom with wax paper. Pour in batter.

Mix 1/3 cup sugar with the chopped nuts and chocolate chips. Sprinkle over top of cake before baking. Bake at 350°F for about 40 minutes, or until toothpick inserted in center of cake comes out clean.

Serves 20.

RED DEVIL CAKE

A rich reddish brown color

        unsweetened chocolate--2 squares (2 oz.)
        water--1/2 cup
        cake flour--2 cups, sifted
        baking soda--1 teaspoon
        salt--1/4 teaspoon
        butter--1/2 cup
        sugar--1-1/2 cups
        eggs--3 large
        buttermilk--1 cup
        vanilla--1 teaspoon

Melt the chocolate with the water and stir until thick.
Sift the flour with the soda and salt. Cream butter and
sugar until light and fluffy. Add the eggs, one at a time,
to the sugar mixture. Beat well. Fold in flour and milk
alternately until well blended. Add chocolate and vanilla
and mix well. Pour into 2 well greased round 9" cake tins.
Bake at 350°F for 30 minutes or until cake just begins to
come away from side of tin.

I added a fudge frosting. Just make up your favorite fudge
recipe, but beat it while still hot. Add 1/2 teaspoon
cream and spread on cake while the fudge is still warm.

ORANGE CAKE

This cake is enjoyed by all

flour--2 cups
baking soda--1 teaspoon
salt--1 teaspoon
orange juice concentrate--6 oz., thawed
sugar--1 cup
butter--3/4 cup, softened
milk--1/2 cup
eggs--2 large
seedless raisins--1 cup
chopped walnuts--1/2 cup

Topping:

sugar--1/3 cup
chopped walnuts--1/4 cup
cinnamon--1 teaspoon

Sift flour, soda, and salt together. Mix with 1/2 cup of
the orange juice concentrate, sugar, butter, milk, and eggs.
Mix at low speed 30 seconds. Beat at medium speed 3 minutes. Fold in raisins and nuts. Pour into well greased
glass 13" x 9" pan. Bake at 350°F for 40 to 45 minutes or
until cake starts to come away from sides of tin.

Drizzle remaining orange juice over warm cake. Mix sugar,
nuts, and cinnamon. Sprinkle over warm cake.

Serves 16.

CHOCOLATE FROSTING

Just like the pastry chefs use on their fancy cakes

        semi-sweet chocolate--10 oz.
        water--3 tablespoons
        egg yolks--4 large
        non-dairy whipping cream--10 oz.
        vanilla--1 teaspoon

Melt chocolate in top of double boiler. Add water. Remove
from heat. Immediately beat in the egg yolks with a wire
whisk or beater. Cool. Whip cream. Add vanilla. When
chocolate cools to room temperature mix with cream. Ice
cake immediately or frosting will not spread well. This
will ice a 3 layer cake.

BANANA CAKE

        banana cake mix--1 pkg. (18 oz.)
        milk--1/4 cup
        eggs--3 large
        butter--1/4 cup
        brown sugar--1/4 cup
        cinnamon--1/2 teaspoon
        nutmeg--1/4 teaspoon
        very ripe bananas--3 medium, mashed
        chopped walnuts--1/4 cup
        semi-sweet chocolate chips--6 oz. pkg.
        powdered sugar--2 tablespoons, sifted

In a large mixing bowl, blend all ingredients except last 3. Beat at medium speed for 4 minutes. Fold in walnuts and chocolate chips. Generously grease and lightly flour bottom and sides of a 13" x 9" pan and bake at 350°F for 35 minutes. Cool. Sprinkle with powdered sugar. Do not refrigerate or freeze! Makes 16 squares.

FRENCH COFFEE CAKE

Even better re-heated

flour--4 cups, sifted
sugar--1-1/4 cups
butter--1/2 cup
salt--1/2 teaspoon
milk--1 cup, warm
egg yolks--3 large
water--1/4 cup, lukewarm
yeast--1 envelope

egg whites--3 large
cinnamon--1 teaspoon
chopped nuts--1 cup

powdered sugar--1/2 cup

Blend flour, 1/4 cup sugar, butter, and salt until mixture is the consistency of coarse sand. Beat egg yolks and add to warm milk. Combine milk and flour mixtures. Add the yeast to the lukewarm water. When yeast is frothy, add to flour mixture. Knead a few minutes. Cover bowl with stretch plastic or any airtight cover. Refrigerate over-night. Dough will double in size.

Beat egg whites until thick. Gradually add 1 cup of sugar. Fold in cinnamon and nuts. Divide dough in half. Roll dough about 1/2" thick in a rectangular shape. Cover each sheet of dough with half of the egg white mixture. Roll each half snugly like a jelly roll. Place on a greased cookie sheet.

Cover and place in a warm, but not hot place for about 1-1/2 hours or until dough rises a little less than double. Bake at 350°F for 45 minutes. Mix powdered sugar with water, a few drops at a time, to form a thick paste. Spread over cake while still hot. Makes 36 slices.

CHERRY COFFEE CAKE

Cherry lovers take notice

flour--1-1/4 cups, sifted
sugar--1/2 cup
baking powder--1-1/2 teaspoons
salt--1/4 teaspoon
butter--1/4 cup
egg--1 large, slightly beaten
milk--3 tablespoons
vanilla--1 teaspoon
cherry pie filling--21 oz. can

Topping:

flour--1/2 cup, sifted
brown sugar--1/4 cup
cinnamon--1/2 teaspoon
butter--4 tablespoons

Sift the flour, sugar, baking powder, and salt together. Cut in butter with blender until mixture resembles coarse crumbs. Combine egg, milk, and vanilla. Add to dry ingredients and mix well. Spread in 10" greased cake pan. Spoon cherry pie filling on top.

For topping, combine flour, brown sugar, cinammon, and butter. Crumble over pie filling. Bake at 350°F for 45 to 50 minutes. Serves 8. Freezes well.

SOUR CREAM CAKE

butter--1/2 cup
sugar--1 cup
eggs--2 large
flour--1-1/2 cups, sifted
baking powder--1-1/2 teaspoons
baking soda--1 teaspoon
sour cream--1/2 pint (1 cup)
vanilla--1 teaspoon
brown sugar--1/4 cup
cinnamon--1 teaspoon
chopped walnuts--1/2 cup
butter--3 tablespoons, melted

Beat butter and sugar until fluffy. Add eggs beating after each addition. Sift flour with baking powder and baking soda. Add to creamed sugar, alternating with the sour cream. Add vanilla. Pour half of the batter into a well greased 9" x 9" pan. Combine brown sugar with cinnamon, walnuts, and melted butter. Sprinkle half of this mixture over the batter in the pan. Spoon remaining batter over nut mixture and sprinkle remaining nut mixture on top. Bake at 350°F for about 50 minutes or until cake begins to shrink from sides of pan. Serves 10.

OLD FASHIONED HONEY CAKE

The real McCoy

coffee--1 cup
instant coffee--1 teaspoon
cocoa--1 tablespoon
ginger--1/4 teaspoon
nutmeg--1/4 teaspoon
allspice--1/4 teaspoon
cinnamon--1/2 teaspoon
shortening--2 tablespoons
sugar--1 cup
egg yolks--2 large
vanilla--1 teaspoon
honey--1/2 cup
flour--2-1/4 cups
baking powder--1-1/2 teaspoons
baking soda--3/4 teaspoon
chopped walnuts--1/2 cup

Heat coffee with instant coffee, cocoa, ginger, nutmeg, allspice, and cinnamon. Cool.

Combine shortening, sugar, egg yolks, vanilla, and honey. Beat until creamy.

Sift flour, baking powder, and baking soda together. Add to creamy mixture alternating with the coffee. Blend well. Add nuts. Bake in well greased and floured tube pan at 350°F for 45 minutes. Test to see if cake is done. If not, bake another 10 minutes and check again.

Serves 12.

NUT CAKE

What a cake

        flour--1-1/2 cups
        baking powder--1-1/2 teaspoons
        salt--1/8 teaspoon
        sugar--1-1/4 cups
        eggs--6 large, separated, at room temperature
        oil--3 tablespoons
        water--3 tablespoons
        lemon juice--1 teaspoon
        lemon rind--1/2 teaspoon, grated
        walnuts--1 cup, ground

Sift flour, baking powder, and salt together. Set aside.
Cream sugar and egg yolks. Add oil, water, lemon juice,
rind, and nuts. Mix. Add flour. Mix thoroughly.

Beat egg whites until stiff, but not dry. Fold into batter.
Pour into 9" angel food pan. Bake at 350°F for 50 minutes.
Leave in pan until completely cool.

To remove cake, first run spatula along edge and tube; then
around bottom of pan. Serves 12.

SPONGE CAKE

A basic recipe

        eggs--6 large, separated
        cream of tartar--3/4 teaspoon
        sugar--1 cup
        water--1/2 cup
        vanilla--1 teaspoon
        cake flour--1-1/2 cups, sifted
        salt--1/4 teaspoon
        baking powder--1/2 teaspoon

Beat egg whites and cream of tartar together until stiff.
Cream yolks, sugar, water, and vanilla until lemon colored
and fluffy. Sift flour. Measure, then sift flour, salt,
and baking powder together 3 times. Fold flour into yolk
mixture. Then fold in beaten egg whites thoroughly. Pour
into 10" tube pan. Bake at 350°F for 45 to 50 minutes until
it springs back at the touch and is golden.

162

PASSOVER CHOCOLATE CAKE

This is a light and delicious Passover cake

matzo cake meal--1/2 cup
cocoa--4 tablespoons
eggs--6 large, separated
sugar--1 cup
water--2 tablespoons
oil--2 tablespoons
lemon juice--1 teaspoon
chopped walnuts--1/2 cup

Sift cake meal and cocoa together. Beat the egg yolks; gradually add the sugar, beating until thick and light in color. Stir in water, oil, and lemon juice. Mix. Add cake meal and cocoa and mix by hand. Add chopped nuts and mix again. In separate bowl, beat egg whites until stiff; fold into other mixture carefully. Turn into well greased 9" tube pan or 9" x 9" pan. Bake at 350°F for approximately 40 minutes. This cake may be served with whipped cream and bananas. Serves 8.

This cake can be frozen.

GENOISE CAKE

Good for petits fours

eggs--4 large
sugar--9 tablespoons (1/2 cup plus 1 tablespoon)
cake flour--1-1/2 cups, sifted
vanilla--1/2 teaspoon
butter--7 tablespoons, soft (not melted)

Place mixing bowl in pan of hot water. Break eggs into bowl. Beat eggs, gradually adding sugar as you beat. Continue beating for about 10 minutes. Remove bowl from the hot water. Continue beating until batter is cool. (I hope you are using an electric beater.) Carefully fold in sifted flour about 1/3 at a time. With the greatest of care, fold in the very soft butter and vanilla. Pour batter into 9" x 9" well buttered pan. Bake at 340°F for 25 to 30 minutes. Remove cake from oven the second the sides begin to separate from the tin. Cool for 5 minutes. Remove cake from tin and allow to cool on rack. This recipe makes excellent lady fingers.

CANDY CONFETTI TORTE

My husband's very favorite çake - worth the effort

                cake flour--1-1/2 cups, sifted
                sugar--1-1/2 cups
                egg yolks--8 large (1/2 cup)
                cold water--1/4 cup
                lemon juice--1 tablespoon
                vanilla--1 teaspoon
                egg whites--8 large (1 cup)
                cream of tartar--1 teaspoon
                salt--1 teaspoon

Sift flour and 3/4 cup sugar into a bowl. Make a well in
mixture. Add the egg yolks, cold water, lemon juice, and
vanilla into well. Beat until very smooth. Beat egg whites
slightly, add the salt and cream of tartar. Beat until soft
peaks form. Gradually add 3/4 cup sugar, 2 tablespoons at a
time. Beat until whites are stiff and stand up in peaks.
Fold first mixture carefully into second. Pour into ungreased 10" tube pan. Bake at 350°F for 50 to 55 minutes or
until cake springs back when touched. Invert pan 1 hour or
until cool. Remove and split into 4 layers.

164

Filling and Frosting:

heavy cream--3 cups
powdered sugar--4 tablespoons
vanilla--2 teaspoons

Whip the cream and add the sugar and vanilla. Spread 1/2
between layers. Spread the rest over top and sides.

Honeycomb Topping:

sugar--1-1/2 cups
instant coffee--1/4 teaspoon
light corn syrup--1/4 cup
hot water--1/4 cup
baking soda--1 tablespoon, sifted

Combine sugar, coffee, syrup, and water in large sauce pan.
Cook to hard crack (290°F). Remove from heat immediately
and add the soda. Stir vigorously only until mixture becomes frothy. Pour foamy mixture into ungreased shallow
metal pan. Do not spread or stir. Let stand until cool.
Knock out of pan. Crush between wax paper with rolling pin.
Gingerly spread the crushed brittle onto the sides and top
of the cake. Add this topping just before serving. This
cake is almost the same as that expensive one made by a San
Francisco candy company. Delicious. Serves 12. Do not
freeze.

CHIFFON HONEY CAKE

A holiday cake

coffee--2/3 cup, strong, plus 1 tablespoon instant coffee
baking soda--1 teaspoon
eggs--6 large, separated
cream of tartar--1/2 teaspoon
baking powder--1 teaspoon
flour--2 cups
sugar--1/2 cup
walnuts--3/4 cup, finely ground
honey--1 cup
oil--1/2 cup
cinnamon--1/2 teaspoon
cloves--1/2 teaspoon, ground
nutmeg--1/2 teaspoon
salt--1/4 teaspoon

Add baking soda to coffee. Set aside. Beat egg whites until stiff, adding cream of tartar while beating. Mix all
ingredients except egg whites together. When mixture is
smooth, carefully fold in whites. Pour batter into ungreased angel pan. Bake at 350°F for 1 hour or until a
toothpick comes clean when inserted in center. Do not over
bake. Invert tin and place center piece on cup or glass.
Cool before removing from tin. Serves 12.

PASSOVER BANANA CAKE

An old family recipe

eggs--8 large, separated
sugar--1 cup
banana--1 large, mashed
orange juice--1/2 cup
orange rind--1 teaspoon, grated
lemon juice--2 tablespoons
lemon rind--1/4 teaspoon, grated
matzo cake meal--3/4 cup
potato starch--1/4 cup
chopped walnuts--1 cup

Topping:

sugar--3 tablespoons
egg white--1 large

Pre-heat oven to 350°F for 1/2 hour.

Place egg whites in large bowl and beat until frothy. Gradually add 3/4 cup sugar until whites resemble marshmallows.
In a second bowl, beat egg yolks and 1/4 cup sugar until
pale yellow. Add yolks to egg whites using mixer.

Mash banana. Add rind and juices. Mix thoroughly. This
should make 1-1/4 cups. If it doesn't, add more banana.
Add to egg mixture. Gradually add cake meal and starch.
Mix well. Fold in nuts. Pour into ungreased, warm tube pan
and place in center of oven. Bake at 350°F for 50 to 55 minutes.

Put warm cake rack on terry towel away from a draft. Turn
cake pan over onto cake rack. Cool completely before removing from pan.

Prepare topping just before serving. Add sugar to slightly
beaten egg white. Continue beating until stiff. Frost.
Serve with fresh strawberries.

ALMOND TORTE

An old fashioned torte

    almonds--1/2 lb., ground (2 cups)
    powdered sugar--2 cups, sifted
    eggs--8 large, separated
    cream of tartar--1 teaspoon
    salt--1/4 teaspoon
    coffee--3 tablespoons plus 1/4 teaspoon instant coffee
    cream--8 oz., whipped and sweetened

Pre-heat oven to 325°F. Grease cake tube. Beat egg whites
slightly. Add cream of tartar and salt. Continue beating
until whites are stiff, but not dry. Set aside. Beat egg
yolks slightly. Add sugar. Continue beating until thick.
Alternating with nuts, fold yolks carefully into whites.
Pour into cake tube. Bake for 20 minutes. Reduce heat to
300°F and bake for at least 1 hour. Do not peek before.
Turn off oven, open door, leave cake in oven for 1 more hour.

Mix whipped cream with coffee and serve with torte.

Serves about 8.

DELUXE CHEESE CAKE

I thought that I could never bake
Half so beautiful a cake.
        I was tempted to buy it,
         But finally I tried it
And found it was cinchy to make.

Crust:

zwieback crumbs--1-1/2 cups
butter--1/2 cup
sugar--1/3 cup
coconut--4 oz.
chopped almonds--1/2 cup

Mix ingredients well. Press into sides and bottom of a spring form.

Filling:

eggs--6 large, separated
sugar--1 cup
cream cheese--1-1/2 lbs.
lemon rind--1/2 teaspoon, grated
cherry pie filling--10 oz.

Beat yolks until light and fluffy. Gradually add 1/2 cup of sugar. Beat until thick.

Mash cream cheese with a fork. Add half of egg yolk mixture. Blend well. Add the rest of the egg yolk mixture and beat until smooth. Add lemon rind and blend.

Beat egg whites until thick. Gradually add 1/2 cup of sugar. Continue beating until whites stand up in peaks. Fold into egg yolks and cream cheese.

Pour into the prepared crust. Bake at 300°F for 50 to 60 minutes. Remove from oven and allow to cool. Remove sides of spring form. Cover with pie filling. Serves 12.

Whipped cottage cheese may be substituted for the cream cheese. You lose some of the flavor and 140 calories per serving.

RAINBOW PARTY CAKE

A sight to behold

```
angel food cake--1 round 10" ready made
vanilla ice cream--1 pint
chocolate ice cream--1 pint
raspberry ice cream--1 pint
strawberry ice cream--1 quart
cookie crumbs--3 tablespoons
shredded coconut--3 oz., toasted
```

Allow ice cream to soften slightly. Slice cake width-wise, making 4 separate rings. Remove 3 top rings. Spread 1 pint ice cream over bottom layer. Add another cake ring and repeat twice. Ice the entire cake with the quart of ice cream. Re-freeze.

Remove from freezer about 5 minutes before serving. Top with cookie crumbs and toasted shredded coconut. Serves 12.

Low cholesterol if you substitute sherbet for ice cream.

BUTTERED WALNUT CAKE

For a coffee klatch

        butter--3/4 cup
        sugar--2-1/2 cups
        eggs--4 large, separated
        cake flour--3 cups, sifted
        baking powder--2 teaspoons
        milk--1 cup
        melted butter--6 tablespoons
        cinnamon--1 tablespoon
        chopped nuts--1/2 cup

Cream butter and 2 cups sugar until fluffy. Beat egg yolks
until creamy. Fold into creamed sugar and butter.

Sift flour and baking powder. Add to batter alternately
with the milk.

Beat egg whites and fold carefully into cake. Pour into
well greased spring form. Mix 1/2 cup sugar with cinnamon
and nuts. Spread over top of cake. Spoon melted butter
evenly over the top. Bake at 350°F for 1 hour. Remove
from pan while still hot.

Serves 12.

FRUIT JELLY SQUARES

An unusually good Passover cake

    eggs--4 large, separated (at room temperature)
    salt--1/16 teaspoon
    sugar--3/4 cup
    lemon juice--2 tablespoons
    orange juice--4 tablespoons
    matzo cake meal--6 tablespoons
    potato starch--2 tablespoons
    fresh lemon rind--2 tablespoons, grated
    coconut macaroons--8 crumbled
    jam--1/2 cup (your favorite)
    powdered sugar--2 tablespoons

Beat egg whites until soft peaks form. Gradually add salt
and then sugar and continue to beat. Slowly add lemon
juice, orange juice, and egg yolks. Mix again. Mix cake
meal and potato starch together and add to above mixture.
Add lemon rind and macaroons and mix thoroughly. Pour into
9" x 11" pan lined with wax paper and greased with butter.
Bake at 350°F for 20 minutes or until cake springs back when
touched. When cool, invert onto a plate. Remove wax paper
carefully. Cut cake into 2 layers. Spread jam on bottom
half and replace top layer. Sift powdered sugar over top.
Makes 20 squares.

THE REBBETZIN'S CAKE

Excellent texture and flavor

butter--1/2 cup
sugar--1 cup
eggs--2 large
flour--2 cups, sifted
baking powder--1 teaspoon
baking soda--1 teaspoon
sour cream--1/2 pint (1 cup)
vanilla--1 teaspoon
semi-sweet chocolate chips--1/2 cup
dark brown sugar--1/4 cup, firmly packed
chopped walnuts--1/4 cup
cinnamon--1 teaspoon
fine dry bread crumbs

Cream butter and sugar. Add eggs and beat until fluffy.
Sift flour, baking powder, and baking soda together. Add
flour to batter alternating with sour cream. Stir in vanilla and chocolate chips.

Grease a 10" tube pan and coat with the bread crumbs. Spoon
batter evenly into the pan. It will form a rather shallow
layer. Combine the brown sugar, nuts, and cinnamon and
press this mixture evenly into the surface of the batter.
Bake at 350°F for 45 minutes. Invert, at once, onto a dish.
Turn again and cool.

Serves 10.

"I have eaten my honeycomb with my honey." (Song of Songs)

POUND CAKE

        cake flour--2-1/4 cups, sifted
        baking powder--1/2 teaspoon
        salt--1/2 teaspoon
        butter--1 cup
        sugar--1-1/3 cups
        vanilla--1 teaspoon
        almond extract--1-1/2 teaspoons
        eggs--4 large
        milk--1/3 cup

Sift flour, baking powder, and salt together. Cream butter and sugar until very light and fluffy. Add flavorings. Add eggs 1 at a time. Beat 1 minute after each addition.

Add flour to batter alternately with the milk. Beat at medium speed for 2 minutes.

Butter a 4" x 9" loaf pan. Line the bottom with a piece of wax paper. Pour batter into pan. Bake at 325°F for 70 to 80 minutes. Remove from oven as soon as the edges start to break away from the edge of pan. Allow to cool 10 minutes and invert onto a cake rack.

Double the recipe if using a large bundt pan.

                    DIVINE FILLING FOR POUND CAKE

        semi-sweet chocolate chips--2 oz.
        orange liqueur--3 tablespoons
        chopped walnuts--3 tablespoons
        ricotta cheese--1 lb.
        sugar--1/4 cup

Mix ingredients in blender. Cut a 4" x 9" pound cake lengthwise into 4 layers. Fill each layer with filling and reassemble.

                    ****

"Thou didst eat fine flour and honey and oil." (Ezekiel)

FROSTING FOR POUND CAKE

```
        semi-sweet chocolate chips--10 oz.
        water--1/4 cup
        whipping cream--1/2 cup
        instant coffee--1 tablespoon
        unsalted butter--3/4 cup
```

Melt chocolate chips and water in top of double boiler. Add cream and coffee. Stir until mixture is well blended. Cut chilled butter into 6 pieces. Stir into mixture 1 at a time. Chill until thick enough to spread, about 1/2 hour.

Frost outside of filled 4" x 9" pound cake.

ROCKY ROAD CAKE

Delicious frozen or thawed

```
    semi-sweet chocolate chips--12 oz.
    sugar--1/4 cup
    eggs--4 large, separated
    vanilla--1 teaspoon
    whipping cream--1 pint (16 oz.)
    angel food cake--10" round, torn into bite size pieces
    walnuts--1 cup chopped
```

Melt chocolate chips in a double boiler. Add sugar. Mix in yolks slowly. Mix thoroughly. Add vanilla and remove from heat. Beat whites until stiff but not dry. Beat cream until it forms soft peaks.

Fold egg whites into chocolate mixture. Then fold in whipped cream.

Grease a 10" spring type angel food pan. Cover bottom with 1/3 of cake. Add layer of 1/3 of chocolate and 1/3 of nuts Repeat twice using up all of the ingredients. Keep in refrigerator overnight. Unmold and freeze until served. Let it set out 5 minutes before serving.

Serves 12.

****

"With a table prepared before it." (Ezekiel)

HIGH VITAMIN CAKE

Vitamin A a plenty

butter--1/2 cup
brown sugar--1 cup
eggs--2 large
carrots--2 cups, grated (about 6 large carrots)
cake flour--1 cup
baking powder--1 teaspoon
salt--1/2 teaspoon
ginger--1/2 teaspoon
nutmeg--1/2 teaspoon

Cream butter and sugar well. Add eggs, 1 at a time, beating after each addition. Fold in carrots. Continue beating until fluffy.

Sift dry ingredients. Fold into batter a little at a time. Bake in well greased mold at 325°F for 1 hour.

Serves 6.

Nice for a company dinner.

CARROT CAKE

What an aroma while baking

baking soda--2 teaspoons
eggs--3 large, beaten
sugar--2 cups
cinnamon--1 teaspoon
vanilla--2 teaspoons
salt--1 teaspoon
oil--1-1/4 cups
flour--2 cups, sifted
coconut--3-1/2 oz. can
carrots--2 cups, shredded
chopped nuts--1 cup
crushed pineapple--1 cup, fruit and juice

Hand mix all ingredients until well blended. Bake in glass 9" x 13" baking dish at 350°F for 50 minutes. Do not over-bake. Cool and cut into squares. Serves 20.

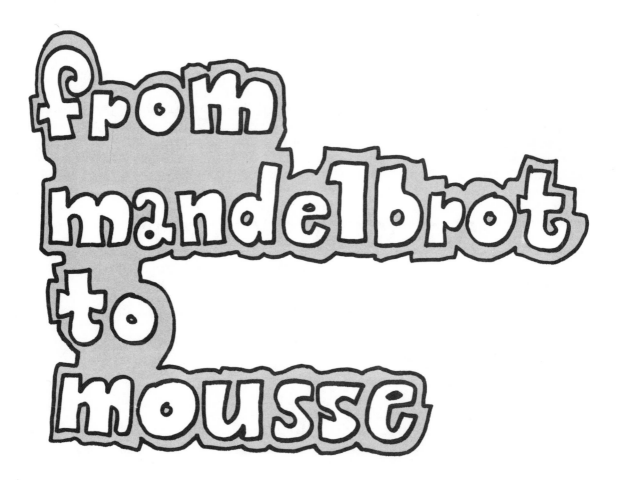

from mandelbrot to mousse

MERINGUE COOKIES

This is an office favorite

        pitted dates--1 lb., cut in quarters
        walnuts--1-1/2 cups, large pieces
        flour--1 tablespoon
        egg whites--4 large
        powdered sugar--2 cups, sifted before measuring
        orange rind--1/2 teaspoon, grated

Cut dates with scissors. Mix with flour to keep dates from
sticking together. Mix with nuts. Set aside. Beat egg
whites until foamy. Gradually beat in powdered sugar until
egg whites are stiff. Fold this mixture into dates and nuts.
Grease cookie sheet. By teaspoon drop mixture 2" apart onto
a cookie sheet. Sprinkle each mound with orange rind. Bake
at 325°F for 25 minutes. Cool 2 to 3 minutes. Remove from
pan.

NUT KAMISH BROT

These are like your grandmother used to make

        eggs--3 large
        oil--1 cup
        sugar--1 cup plus 1 tablespoon
        flour--3-1/2 cups
        baking powder--2 teaspoons
        salt--3/4 teaspoon
        vanilla--1 teaspoon
        chopped walnuts--1 cup
        semi-sweet chocolate chips--3 oz., chopped
        cocoa--1 tablespoon
        cinnamon--1 teaspoon
        slivered almonds--4 oz.

Beat eggs well and add oil and 1 cup sugar. Sift dry ingredients and add to egg mixture. Add vanilla, walnuts, and
chocolate chips. Shape into 4 rolls and bake on cookie
sheet at 350°F for 25 minutes. Slice while warm and sprinkle with mixture of 1 tablespoon sugar, cocoa, cinnamon, and
almonds. Return to oven at 225°F and bake for another 15
minutes.

Makes 80 cookies. Freezes well.

CHOCOLATE MERINGUES

A beauty on your cookie tray

    egg whites--4 large, at room temperature
    sugar--1 cup
    vanilla--1/2 teaspoon
    unsweetened chocolate--2 oz. (2 squares), grated
    semi-sweet chocolate chips--6 oz.
    milk--1/4 cup
    walnuts--1 cup, finely chopped

Beat egg whites until stiff, but not dry; gradually add 2/3
cup sugar while continuing to beat. Add vanilla. Gradually
fold in remaining 1/3 cup sugar and finely grated chocolate.
Shape into ovals from a well rounded teaspoon. Place on
teflon baking sheet or one covered with brown paper. Bake
in slow oven at 275°F for 45 to 50 minutes. Remove from pan.
Melt chocolate chips with milk in top of double boiler. Dip
top of cool meringue in warm chocolate and then in chopped
nuts.

Will make 50 cookies.

PASSOVER MANDELBROT

Even prettier than those not made for Passover

        eggs--6 large
        sugar--1-1/2 cups
        oil--1-1/2 cups
        chopped almonds--1 cup
        matzo meal--1 cup
        matzo cake meal--1 cup
        potato flour--1 tablespoon
        cinnamon--1 tablespoon

Mix all ingredients in order listed and refrigerate for 2
hours until it thickens. On a cookie sheet place two 6" x
14" heavy aluminum foil sheets. Fold up 1" on all sides,
pinching corners together to form 2 baking tins. (Mixture
is not thick enough to stand alone.) Fill each "tin" with
1/2 the batter. Bake at 350°F for 30 minutes or until cake
tester comes out clean. Remove mandelbrot from foil. Cut
into 1/2" slices and brown at 350°F for 10 minutes on each
side. Makes 5 dozen cookies.

RUSSIAN PIE BARS

Beautiful to look at

butter--1 cup, softened
sugar--1 cup
egg yolks--6 large
almond extract--1 teaspoon
flour--2-1/2 cups, sifted

Topping:

apricot jam--24 oz.   (do not use jelly)
egg whites--6 large
salt--1/8 teaspoon
sugar--1 cup
walnuts--8 oz., finely chopped

In a large bowl, cream shortening and sugar. Add egg yolks
and flavoring. Mix thoroughly. Add flour gradually and mix
again.

In an 11" x 16" ungreased cookie pan, pat dough firmly and
evenly. Spread with jam. Beat egg whites slightly. Add
salt and gradually add sugar. Beat until stiff. Fold in
nuts gently. Spread this mixture over jam.

Bake at 350°F for 45 minutes. When cold, cut in finger size
slices and remove. Makes about 75 cookies.

CHERRY NUT KAMISH BROT

A colorful and tasty cookie

flour--3 cups, sifted
salt--1/2 teaspoon
baking powder--2 teaspoons
eggs--3 large
oil--3/4 cup
sugar--1 cup
vanilla--1 teaspoon
chopped nuts--1/2 cup
poppy seeds--1/4 cup
semi-sweet chocolate chips--6 oz.
maraschino cherries--8 oz. jar

Sift flour, salt, and baking powder together. Beat eggs, oil, sugar, and vanilla together. Add dry ingredients and mix well. Add nuts, poppy seeds, and chocolate chips and mix again. Cut cherries in eighths and mix in carefully. Roll into 4" thick "sausages" and bake on greased cookie sheet at 350°F for 30 minutes. Slice while warm. Freezes well. Makes 8 dozen cookies.

HUNGARIAN APPLE STRUDEL

Even Zsa Zsa would like these

green baking apples--2 large, peeled and sliced
6 strudel leaves--about 1/3 lb., 15" x 24"
sugar--2 tablespoons
cinnamon--1 teaspoon
seedless raisins--1 cup
chopped pecans--1/2 cup
butter--1/2 cup, melted
cream--2 teaspoons
bread crumbs--1/4 cup

For strudel leaves use the prepared filo dough which may be purchased at a specialty delicatessen; or make your own using the recipe for Stretched Strudel Dough.

Lay out 2 strudel leaves on a large clean dish towel. Brush top side of dough with the melted butter.

Cover apples with sugar and cinnamon. Mix with raisins and pecans. Spoon 1/3 of fruit in a line along the long side of the dough. Sprinkle remaining surface of dough lightly with the bread crumbs. Roll up dough starting with the end that is fruited. Bend back a little of the dough at each side to keep in the juices. Continue to roll up. Place folded side down on buttered cookie sheet. Brush dough with cream to brown well. Continue as above until fruit is used up. Bake at 325°F about 30 to 40 minutes. Remove from oven. Run a spatula under roll before it cools to prevent sticking. Cut in diagonal 1" slices with a serrated knife.

Makes about 30 slices.

"Stay ye me with dainties, refresh me with apples." Song of Songs)

179

HAMENTASCHEN FOR PURIM

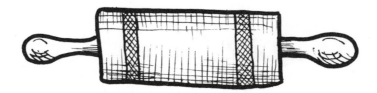

Apricot, prune, or poppy - they're all good

flour--2-1/2 cups, sifted
salt--1/2 teaspoon
sugar--3 tablespoons
butter--1 cup, softened
egg yolks--3 large
white vinegar--3 tablespoons
cold water--3 tablespoons
poppy seed, prune or apricot filling--2 cans (12 oz. each)
chopped walnuts--1/2 cup
lemon juice--1 tablespoon

Combine 1-1/2 cups flour, salt, sugar, and butter, rubbing
butter into flour with fingers. Beat egg yolks lightly with
fork. Add vinegar and water. Sift remaining 1 cup flour
into egg mixture and mix lightly. Combine both mixtures
blending well with a fork. Cover and refrigerate overnight.
Pinch off marble size pieces of dough and roll each on a
floured surface to a 2-1/2" round.

Mix thoroughly fruit filling, walnuts, and lemon juice.
Place a teaspoon of filling in the center of each round.
Pinch edges together to form a triangle and seal in filling.
Place on an ungreased cookie sheet. Bake at 400°F for 20
minutes or until lightly brown.

Freezes well. Makes about 2-1/2 dozen.

MANDELBROT

You say, "mandelbread," and I say, "mandelbrot"

            flour--3 cups
            salt--1/2 teaspoon
            baking powder--2 teaspoons
            eggs--3 large
            sugar--1 cup
            oil--1 cup
            vanilla--1 teaspoon
            slivered almonds--1 cup
            shredded coconut--1 cup

Sift flour, salt, and baking powder together. Beat eggs.
Mix all ingredients together. Shape dough into 2 long
strips about 14" long and 2" wide and 1" high. Place on
well greased cookie sheet. Bake at 350°F for about 25 to 30
minutes or until brown. Remove pan from oven. Cut cookies
into 1/2" slices and brown at 350°F 10 minutes on each side.

NUT WALKAWAYS

They don't really have feet

            dry yeast--1 pkg.
            lukewarm water--1/4 cup
            flour--2 cups, sifted
            salt--1/8 teaspoon
            butter--3/4 cup
            egg--1 large
            cream cheese--4 oz., softened
            sugar--1/2 cup
            lemon peel--1/2 teaspoon, grated
            chopped walnuts--1/2 cup
            powdered sugar--2 tablespoons

Soften yeast in water. Set aside. Combine flour and salt.
Cut in butter. Add yeast and egg. Mix until just blended.
Divide dough in half. Roll out into two 13" x 9" rectangles.
Mix cream cheese, sugar, lemon peel, and nuts together.
Spread on rectangles. Roll in jelly roll fashion starting
with long side. On lightly greased cookie sheet place rolls
seam side down. Pinch ends. Cut each strip halfway through
lengthwise. Bake at 375°F for 20 to 25 minutes. Sprinkle
with powdered sugar. Cut into 1" slices. These freeze well.
Makes 26 to 30 cookies.

CITRUS BARS

A gourmet cookie

    butter--1/2 cup, soft enough to cut
    flour--1 cup
    powdered sugar--1/4 cup, sifted

    eggs--2 large, slightly beaten
    sugar--1 cup
    lemon juice--3 tablespoons
    lemon rind--1/2 teaspoon, grated
    baking powder--1/2 teaspoon
    salt--1/2 teaspoon

    powdered sugar--1 tablespoon (for decoration)

Cut butter into flour and powdered sugar. Spread on greased
9" pan. Bake at 350°F for 20 minutes.

Mix eggs, sugar, lemon juice, lemon rind, baking powder, and
salt together. Use a blender if available. Pour into baked
crust. Bake at 350°F for 25 minutes or until top feels dry
to the touch. Cut into 1" squares while warm. Dust with
powdered sugar.

Makes about 75 cookies.

KICHLACH

Easy to make and tastier than bakery products

            eggs--3 large
            salt--1/4 teaspoon
            sugar--5 teaspoons
            oil--1/2 cup
            flour--1-1/4 cups

Beat eggs until light. Then beat in salt, sugar, and oil.
Beat in flour gradually until very smooth. Mixture has a
tendency to get caught up in beaters as the flour is added.
Drop by teaspoon onto a greased baking sheet, leaving about
2" between each cookie. Cookies will spread and puff in
baking. Bake at 325°F for 20 to 25 minutes or until golden
brown. Makes about 2 dozen cookies.

SCOTTISH SHORTBREAD

My Scotch friend gave me this recipe

flour--4 cups
butter--2 cups
sugar--1 cup

Mix ingredients well, forcing flour and sugar into butter with your impeccably clean hands. Shape into 3 balls. Press each ball onto a buttered cookie sheet with the palm of your hand. Form round discs about 5" across. Prick well with a fork. Bake at 325°F for 20 minutes, but do not allow to brown. Remove from oven. Cut immediately into 8 pie shaped pieces, but do not remove from tin until cool. These taste the way you always hope your cookies are going to taste.

Makes 16 large cookies.

PECAN PRETTIES

butter--1 cup
cream cheese--3 oz., softened
sugar--1 cup
egg--1 large
almond extract--1 teaspoon
flour--2-1/2 cups, sifted
salt--1/2 teaspoon
baking soda--1/4 teaspoon
egg white--1 large
pecans--1 cup, finely chopped

canned chocolate icing--1/2 cup
pecan halves--2 oz.

Cream butter and cream cheese. Add sugar, egg, and extract. Sift dry ingredients together and stir into creamed mixture. Chill dough. Form into 1" balls. Roll in egg white and then into finely chopped nuts. Place on ungreased cookie sheet about 3" apart. Bake at 350°F 10 to 15 minutes.

Cool. Place 1/2 teaspoon icing on each cookie and put a pecan half on top. Yield 4-1/2 dozen.

HORNS

A unique addition for that cookie platter

        butter--1 cup
        pecans--1/2 cup, chopped fine
        sugar--1/4 cup
        vanilla--1/2 teaspoon
        flour--2 cups

Mix all ingredients together well. Shape 1 teaspoon of dough
at a time like a horn. This is a solid cookie, not hollow.
Bake at 350°F for about 15 minutes. Dip large end in colored
cake frosting.

MOCK STRUDEL

I'll take this over the real thing any day

    butter--1 cup, softened
    sour cream--1/2 pint (1 cup) or cream cheese--1/2 lb.
    flour--2 cups
    salt--1/2 teaspoon
    apricot preserves--1 cup
    coconut--1 cup
    chopped nuts--1 cup
    raisins--1 cup
    powdered sugar--2 tablespoons

Cream butter and sour cream or cream cheese together. Add
flour and salt, using a fork. Mix well. Knead into a ball.
Wrap in waxed paper and refrigerate overnight.

Cut into 4 parts and roll each one on wellfloured board to
10" x 15" size. Cover each with preserves, coconut, nuts,
and raisins. Roll from the 15" side. Pinch ends carefully
and lift to a greased cookie sheet.

Bake at 350°F for 45 minutes until dough is golden and bottom has a hard crust. Remove from pan to cool. Cut into 1"
or 1-1/2" slices. Sprinkle with powdered sugar.

For variety, substitute your favorite preserves.

STRETCHED STRUDEL DOUGH

```
flour--3 cups, sifted
salt--1/4 teaspoon
baking powder--1/4 teaspoon
eggs--2 large
oil--3 teaspoons
lukewarm water--2/3 cup
```

Sift flour, salt, and baking powder into a bowl. Make a well in the center and drop eggs, oil, and water into it. Work into flour, mixing until dough leaves sides of bowl.

Knead dough for 10 minutes or until very smooth and elastic. Divide dough in 3 parts before rolling; makes 3 strudels.

Place warm bowl over dough and let it rest for 1 hour. For next step, you will need a large surface such as a kitchen table. Cover table with cloth; sprinkle with flour.

Roll out dough as thin as you can. Flour your hands. Using the back of your hands under the dough, gently pull it toward you, stretching it as you pull. As the dough stretches, move around the table so that you will not put too much strain on any one part of the dough. Stretch until dough is transparent. You will have a large circle. Brush with oil. It is now ready to use for any recipe calling for strudel dough.

185

ALLIGATOR SQUARES

Another gourmet cookie

    butter--1 cup, softened
    sugar--1 cup
    egg--1 large, separated
    flour--2 cups
    cinnamon--1 teaspoon
    chopped pecans--1 cup

Cream butter and sugar together until smooth. Add egg yolk
and mix thoroughly. Sift flour. Measure and sift again
with cinnamon. Add flour to creamed mixture. Do not use
mixer. Blend together lightly, but thoroughly. Spread in
an even layer over entire surface of a greased 10" x 15"
cookie sheet. Smooth surface with the palms of your hands.
Beat egg white until frothy and cover top of batter completely.

Press nuts evenly into dough.

Bake at 275°F for 50 minutes. While still hot, cut into
1-1/2" squares. Remove and cool. Yields 6 dozen cookies.

CHINESE CHEWS

Delicious chewy squares

    butter--1/2 cup
    sugar--1 cup
    eggs--2 large
    vanilla--1 teaspoon
    flour--1/2 cup
    unsweetened chocolate--2 oz. (2 squares), melted
    chopped nuts--1 cup
    pitted dates--1 cup, chopped

Cream butter and sugar. Beat in eggs 1 at a time. Add vanilla. Mix in flour and chocolate and blend well but do not
over beat. Add dates and nuts.

Pour into a well-buttered 9" x 12" pan. Bake at 350°F for
20 minutes. Do not over bake! Cut into squares and remove
from pan while still warm.

186

JOLLY JELLY BALLS

These simple cookies will dress up any dessert platter

    flour--2 cups, sifted
    egg yolks--2 large
    brown sugar--1/2 cup, packed
    vanilla--1 teaspoon
    butter--1 cup
    egg white--1 large, slightly beaten
    walnuts--1/4 cup, ground
    jelly--1/8 cup

Mix flour, egg yolks, brown sugar, vanilla, and butter together until smooth. Form dough into 1" balls. Roll balls
in egg white and then in ground walnuts. Place on well
greased cookie sheet and bake at 325°F for 5 minutes. Remove from oven and make indentation in the center of each
cookie with the ball of your thumb. Return to oven and bake
20 minutes longer (25 minutes total). Cool and put small
amount of jelly in each depression. These cookies freeze
well.

5 dozen cookies.

DATE AND NUT BARS

Add interest to any cookie tray

    eggs--3 large
    sugar--1 cup
    flour--1 cup, sifted
    baking powder--1 teaspoon
    chopped walnuts--1 cup
    pitted dates--1 cup, cut up, firmly packed
    currants--1/2 cup, dried

Beat eggs in a bowl. Add sugar. Mix well. Add flour and
baking powder. Blend in walnuts, dates, and currants. Mix
thoroughly.

Grease a 10" x 15" pan. Spread batter in pan. Bake at 350°F
for 20 to 25 minutes or until sides pull away from pan and
top springs back when touched. Cut into squares while warm.
Makes 50 bars.

MARK'S FAVORITE BROWNIES

We think of Mark every time we make these

        Dutch chocolate--4 oz.
        butter--1/2 cup
        sugar--3/4 cup
        eggs--2 large
        flour--3/4 cup
        salt--1/8 teaspoon
        baking powder--2 teaspoons
        vanilla--1 teaspoon
        chopped nuts--1/2 cup

Melt chocolate over hot water. Cream butter and sugar. Add
eggs and beat well. Sift flour with salt and baking powder.
Add to creamed mixture. Add chocolate, vanilla, and nuts.
Mix thoroughly. Pour into a well greased 9" x 9" pan. Bake
at 350°F for 25 minutes. Do not over bake. Cut while warm.

Makes 16 squares.

OATMEAL COOKIES

Children will love them!

        raisins--1 cup
        water--1 cup
        butter--3/4 cup, softened
        brown sugar--3/4 cup, firmly packed
        granulated sugar--1/3 cup
        egg--1 large
        vanilla--2 teaspoons
        flour--1 cup, sifted
        salt--1 teaspoon
        baking soda--1/2 teaspoon
        chopped walnuts--1 cup
        coconut--1/3 cup
        semi-sweet chocolate chips--3/4 cup
        oatmeal--3 cups, non-instant

Pre-heat oven to 350°F. Place raisins and cold water in saucepan and bring to a boil. Lower heat and simmer for 20 minutes. Cool. Cream shortening. Add both sugars. Beat well. Add egg and vanilla; then raisin and water mixture. Mix thoroughly. Gradually add sifted dry ingredients. Blend well. Add walnuts, coconut, and chocolate chips. Add oatmeal. Mix until thoroughly blended. Drop by teaspoonful onto a greased cookie sheet. Bake for 15 minutes. Remove when bottoms are lightly browned. Cookie tops will harden as they cool. Yield: 6 dozen.

QUICK COMPANY COOKIES

Soooo good!

        graham cracker crumbs--1-1/4 cups
        coconut--2/3 cup, shredded
        semi-sweet chocolate chips--6 oz.
        sweetened condensed milk--14 oz. can

Butter well an 8" x 8" cake pan. Mix all ingredients thoroughly and pour into pan. Bake at 375°F for 25 minutes. Cut into squares and remove immediately!

When cool, dust with powdered sugar.

Makes 20 squares.

NO BAKE BROWNIES

Will be a favorite of anyone who has a preference
for chocolate

        chopped walnuts--1 cup
        graham cracker crumbs--4 cups
        powdered sugar--1/2 cup, sifted
        instant coffee powder--2 tablespoons
        semi-sweet chocolate chips--12 oz.
        evaporated milk--1 cup
        vanilla--1 teaspoon

Combine walnuts, crumbs, and sugar in large bowl. Heat coffee, chocolate, and evaporated milk over low heat stirring
constantly until smoothly blended. Remove from heat. Add
vanilla. Reserve 1/2 cup of chocolate mixture. Mix remaining chocolate with crumb mixture. Spread evenly in well
buttered 9" x 9" pan. Spread reserved chocolate mixture
over top for glaze. Chill until ready to serve. Keep re-
frigerated.

Makes 32 bars.

PASSOVER BROWNIES

As good as the ones made with regular flour

        oil--1/2 cup
        sugar--1 cup
        eggs--3 large
        matzo cake meal--1/2 cup
        cocoa--1/3 cup
        chopped nuts--1/2 cup

Mix together oil and sugar. Add eggs and mix again. Sift
cake meal and cocoa together and add to the mixture. Add
nuts and mix thoroughly. Grease 8" x 8" pan and pour in
batter. Bake at 350°F for about 25 minutes. Cut into
squares while warm. Remove with care as these are fragile.
These may be frozen.

Makes 30 squares.

HALLOWEEN COOKIES

A nice spicy cookie

seedless raisins--3/4 cup
chopped walnuts--3/4 cup
Muscatel wine--1/4 cup
butter--2/3 cup
sugar--1 cup
brown sugar--1/4 cup
vanilla--1 teaspoon
eggs--2 large
stewed pumpkin--1 cup (not pumpkin pie filling)
flour--2-1/2 cups
baking powder--4 teaspoons
salt--1 teaspoon
cinnamon--1/2 teaspoon
nutmeg--1/2 teaspoon
ginger--1/4 teaspoon

Icing:

powdered sugar--1-1/2 cups
butter--2 tablespoons
Muscatel wine--2 tablespoons

Combine raisins and nuts with 1/4 cup wine and set aside.
Cream butter, white sugar, brown sugar, and vanilla until
fluffy. Beat in eggs 1 at a time. Stir in pumpkin. (Don't
worry if it separates.) Sift flour and baking powder with
salt and spices directly into creamed mixture. Add nuts and
raisins. Mix to a moderately stiff dough. Drop by teaspoons onto lightly greased baking sheet. Bake at 375°F for
15 to 18 minutes.

Cool. Prepare icing by mixing powdered sugar, 2 tablespoons
butter, and 2 tablespoons wine together. Spread icing on
cookies.

****

*"He caused manna to rain upon them for food, and gave them
of the corn of heaven." (Psalms)*

CHOCOLATE BROWNIES

Nobody doesn't love these

unsweetened chocolate--2 oz. (2 squares) (or 1/2 cup cocoa)
butter--1/2 cup
sugar--1 cup
eggs--2 large
flour--1/2 cup
vanilla--1 teaspoon
chopped walnuts--1/2 cup
powdered sugar--2 tablespoons

Melt chocolate. Cream butter and sugar well. Add eggs and beat 15 seconds. Add flour and stir well. Add melted chocolate, vanilla, and walnuts.

Put in well buttered 9" x 9" baking dish. Bake at 350°F for 25 minutes. Brownies are finished when center has raised up slightly and is just slightly firm to touch. Do not over-cook. Cut into squares and sprinkle with powdered sugar.

Makes 16 squares.

REFRIGERATOR COOKIES

flour--2 cups
baking powder--1/2 teaspoon
salt--1/2 teaspoon
butter--2/3 cup
sugar--2/3 cup
egg--1 large, beaten
vanilla--1 teaspoon

Sift flour, baking powder, and salt. Cream butter and sugar Add egg and vanilla. Add dry ingredients a little at a time blending thoroughly. Press dough together and shape into a long roll, 1-1/2" in diameter. Wrap tightly in wax paper. Chill at least 6 hours.

Cut into thin slices. Place on ungreased baking sheet. Bake at 400°F for 5 to 8 minutes or until lightly browned.

1 cup ground nuts or 1 cup coconut may be added to dough before baking. A walnut half may be pressed in center of each cookie before baking. Makes 3 dozen cookies.

CORNFLAKE SQUARES

        cornflake crumbs--1-1/2 cups
        sugar--3 tablespoons
        margarine--1/2 cup, melted
        walnuts--1 cup, chopped
        semi-sweet chocolate chips--6 oz.
        coconut--1-1/2 cups, flaked
        sweetened condensed milk--14 oz. can

Measure cornflake crumbs, sugar, and margarine directly into
a 9" x 13" baking pan. Mix thoroughly. Press mixture firmly to bottom of pan forming a crust. Sprinkle evenly with a
layer of walnuts then a layer of chocolate chips and lastly
a layer of coconut. Pour milk evenly over the top. Bake at
350°F for 25 minutes or until lightly brown around edges.
Cool 10 minutes. Cut into squares. Go around edges with a
sharp knife to facilitate removal. Makes 54 squares.

CHEESE BAKE ULTRA

Bake this at your first opportunity - delicious

        butter--1 cup, softened
        sugar--1/2 cup plus 2 tablespoons
        eggs--6 large
        milk--2 cups
        flour--2-1/2 cups
        baking powder--4 teaspoons
        salt--1 teaspoon
        vanilla--1 teaspoon
        jack cheese--1 lb., crumbled

Cream butter and 1/2 cup sugar. Add 4 eggs, 1 at a time,
beating between additions. Sift flour with baking powder and
salt. Add to butter mixture, alternating with 1-1/2 cups of
milk. Pour half of batter into a 3 quart buttered casserole.

Put jack cheese, 1/2 cup milk, 2 tablespoons of sugar, and 2
eggs into blender. Blend until smooth. Pour this mixture
over the cake batter. Add the other half of batter. Bake
at 325°F for 1 hour. Spoon out and serve like a pudding.

Serves 8.

"Is bread corn crushed?" (Isaiah)

STRAWBERRY PIE

Could compete with Farmer's Market

shortening--1/2 cup
flour--1 cup
salt--1/8 teaspoon
orange juice--3 to 4 tablespoons

strawberries--2 baskets, washed and hulled
strawberries--2 cups, mashed
sugar--1 cup
cornstarch--3 tablespoons
lemon juice--1 tablespoon
whipping cream--8 oz., whipped
powdered sugar--2 tablespoons
vanilla--1 tablespoon

Cut shortening into flour and salt until particles are the size of a pea. Add orange juice, 1 tablespoon at a time, tossing with a fork after each addition. Mix very lightly, only until all of flour is moistened and dough almost cleans sides of bowl. Press firmly into a ball and chill. Roll dough 2" larger than pie tin on a floured board. Fit into tin. Pinch edges gently around rim. Prick bottom extremely well with a fork. Bake at 350°F for 12 to 15 minutes. Remove when lightly browned. Cool.

Cook mashed berries with sugar and cornstarch until clear and thickened. Add lemon juice.

Line pie crust with fresh berries, large side down. Cover with strawberry glaze.

Whip cream. Add powdered sugar and vanilla. Spoon over pie. Criss-cross with fork to make design. Serves 6.

CRANBERRY TARTS

These are some of the best tarts ever

small curd cottage cheese--1/2 cup
butter--1/2 cup
flour--1-1/4 cups
whole cranberry sauce--1/2 cup

194

With the exception of cranberry sauce, mix together all in-gredients (by hand or with slow speed of electric mixer) until well blended, but no longer. Wrap dough in plastic and chill in refrigerator for at least 1 hour. Roll dough on well-floured board. Make it as thin as possible, using 1/2 at a time. Cut dough into 3" squares; place about 1 tea-spoon of cranberry sauce in center of each square; bring the 4 corners up and pinch together, forming a sack. Bake at 375°F for 10 or 15 minutes, or until golden. Makes approxi-mately 4 dozen.

CORNFLAKE MACAROONS

The recipe everyone asks for

    egg whites--2 large, at room temperature
    salt--1/8 teaspoon
    sugar--1 cup
    vanilla--1 teaspoon
    cornflakes--2 cups
    chopped nuts--1 cup or 1 cup coconut

Beat egg whites with salt until stiff, but not dry. Gradu-ally add sugar, beating constantly. Add vanilla. Fold in cornflakes and nuts. Drop by teaspoon onto a well greased cookie sheet. Bake at 300°F for 15 to 20 minutes. Makes 3-1/2 dozen.

GRANDMOTHER'S PIE CRUST

    solid shortening--1 cup (not butter)
    flour--2 cups
    salt--1/2 teaspoon
    baking powder--1/8 teaspoon
    ice water--about 1/4 cup

Sift together flour, salt, and baking powder. Cut shorten-ing into flour. When shortening is about the size of a pea, mix in enough ice water so dough forms a ball. Stop once ball is formed and do not over mix. Do not use your fin-gers to mix. Wrap in wax paper and chill at least 30 min-utes before using.

Cut dough in half and roll out on well floured board. Do not overwork. Baking instructions depend on pie recipe you are using.

LEMON MERINGUE PIE

Like your favorite aunt used to make

        cornstarch--5 tablespoons
        sugar--3/4 cup plus 6 tablespoons
        lemon juice--3 tablespoons
        egg yolks--5 large
        lemon rind--1 teaspoon
        9" pie shell
        egg whites--3 large

Mix cornstarch, lemon juice, and 3/4 cup sugar. Add egg
yolks, 1 at a time. Cook over double boiler until thick
enough to coat a spoon. Add lemon rind. Pour into a 9"
pie shell. Beat the 3 egg whites with 6 tablespoons of
sugar to stand in stiff peaks. Spread over lemon filling.
Bake at 325°F about 20 minutes or until brown.

Serves 6.

CHIFFON PUMPKIN PIE

A special request from a son-in-law

        unflavored gelatin--1 envelope (1 oz.)
        warm water--4 tablespoons
        pumpkin--1-1/4 cups, canned
        eggs--3 large, separated
        sugar--1/2 cup
        allspice--1/4 teaspoon
        cinnamon--1/2 teaspoon
        cloves--1/4 teaspoon
        whipping cream--8 oz.
        powdered sugar--2 tablespoons

Dissolve gelatin in warm water. Mix into pumpkin. Set
aside. Beat egg yolks and sugar until golden and thick.
Add to pumpkin mixture. Add spices. Mix. Cook until mixture coats spoon. Cool.

Beat egg whites until stiff. Fold into pumpkin mixture.
Pour into 9" baked pie crust. Chill 6 hours.

Whip cream with powdered sugar and cover pie.

MOCHA NUT IGLOO

This looks like a picture

```
chocolate mocha ice cream--1 quart, softened
chopped walnuts--1/2 cup
whipping cream--8 oz.
powdered sugar--2 tablespoons
sponge cake--7" layer
vanilla--1 teaspoon
peppermint candy--4 oz., crushed
```

Add nuts to softened ice cream. Pour into a 7" rounded bowl and freeze for at least 6 hours. Cut cake to form a 7" round disc. Place on plate and unmold ice cream onto cake. Whip cream. Add sugar and vanilla. Cover ice cream with the whipped cream and carefully cover with candy. Now you will have a beautiful igloo.

Serves 10.

CLASSIC DESSERT

```
blueberry ice cream--1 quart
creme de cassis--6 tablespoons
```

Pour creme de cassis over blueberry ice cream (or your favorite flavor). Decorate with slightly sweetened whipped cream and slivered toasted almonds. Serves 6.

CHOCOLATE PUFFS

I once brought these to a tea.
And when I said they were baked by me
        I was simply astounded
        By being surrounded
And plagued for my prize recipe.

water--1 cup
butter--1/3 cup
salt--1/8 teaspoon
flour--1 cup, sifted
eggs--4 large

vanilla pudding--3-1/2 oz. pkg. (not instant)
milk--2 cups
whipping cream--1/3 cup

unsweetened chocolate--4 oz. (4 squares)
sugar--3/4 cup
water--1/2 cup

In a heavy saucepan, place water, butter and salt. Heat.
When boiling briskly, add flour, all at once. Stir vigorously. Cook, stirring constantly, until mixture forms a
smooth ball which leaves sides of pan clean. Turn into mixing bowl. One at a time, beat in eggs. Beat until mixture
is thick and shiny.

To make large puffs, drop dough by tablespoons onto ungreased baking sheet. Use a teaspoon to make miniatures.
Bake large puffs at 450°F for 15 minutes. Reduce heat to
325°F for 20 minutes. Bake miniatures at 450°F for 15 minutes; 325°F for 10 minutes. Cool. Cut slit in side of each
puff.

Prepare pudding with milk as directed on package. Place
plastic wrap over pudding while cooling to prevent forming
a skin. Whip cream and fold in gently. Fill puffs.

Melt chocolate over hot water. Set aside. Combine sugar
and warm water in saucepan. Mixing constantly, bring to
full, rolling boil. Remove from heat. When lukewarm, blend
in chocolate. Cool, stirring often until thick enough to
spread. Frost puffs.

MEN'S FAVORITE MOUSSE

Chocolate, of course

    semi-sweet chocolate--8 oz.
    sugar--1/4 cup
    strong coffee--2 tablespoons
    eggs--2 large, separated
    imitation vanilla--1 teaspoon
    almond extract--1/8 teaspoon
    whipping cream--12 oz.

In top of double boiler melt sugar and not coffee. Add the chocolate and melt until smooth. Beat the egg yolks into the hot chocolate. Allow to cool just slightly. Beat the egg whites until stiff and add to chocolate mixture. Whip cream and fold into mixture. Pour into individual ramekins or custard dishes and allow to set a few hours. For an elegant dish, double recipe and place in a spring form that has been lined with lady fingers, unmold, and cover with whipped cream.

CHOCOLATE SOUFFLE

For the gourmet

        butter--6 tablespoons
        chocolate--4 oz. (4 squares)
        flour--1/2 cup
        salt--1/4 teaspoon
        milk--2 cups
        sugar--1-1/3 cups plus 1 teaspoon
        eggs--8 large, separated
        vanilla--1 teaspoon
        cream of tartar--1/4 teaspoon

Sprinkle bottom of a souffle dish or casserole with 1 teaspoon sugar. Take a piece of wax paper twice as high as the
casserole. Tie the paper around the middle of the casserole
making a collar, and thus doubling the height of the dish.

Melt butter with chocolate over low heat. Blend. Remove
from heat. Beat in flour, salt, milk, and half of the sugar.
Stir and cook 20 minutes or until thick. Remove from heat.
Blend in egg yolks and vanilla. This mixture can stand for
2 hours before using, but reheat over hot water just before
finishing.

Beat egg whites slightly. Add cream of tartar. Beat until
fluffy. Gradually pour in remaining sugar. Continue beating until it forms moist dripping peaks. Carefully fold in
chocolate mixture. Pour into casserole. Set in pan of
water. Bake at 425°F for 15 minutes. Reduce heat to 375°F
and continue cooking for 45 minutes or until set.

Serve hot with softened ice cream. Serves 8.

ICE CREAM SURPRISE

        vanilla ice cream--1 gallon
        frozen lemonade--6 oz. concentrate, thawed
        apricot marmalade--12 oz. jar

Soften ice cream slightly. Mix with lemonade and apricot
marmalade. Pour into plastic containers; cover tightly.
Re-freeze until needed.

HAWAIIAN DELIGHT

A delicious as well as nutritious dessert

    eggs--2 large
    whipped cottage cheese--1/2 lb.
    butter--4 tablespoons, melted
    sour cream--1/2 pint (1 cup)
    crushed pineapple--8 oz. can, undrained
    sugar--3 tablespoons
    raisins--1/4 cup
    cornflakes--2 cups slightly crushed

Topping:

    cornflakes--1/2 cup slightly crushed
    cinnamon--1/4 teaspoon
    butter--1/2 tablespoon, softened
    sugar--1/2 teaspoon

Whip eggs. Add all ingredients except topping. Blend until
smooth. Butter a 9" cake pan. Put in a layer of cornflakes;
add 1/2 of the pudding mixture. Add another layer of cornflakes, and finally the rest of pudding mixture. Mix topping ingredients together and sprinkle over pudding. Bake
at 350°F for 30 minutes until mixture is firm and golden.
Serve warm.

Serves 8.

STRAWBERRIES SUPREME

Makes a dish of plain strawberries into company dessert

        frozen raspberries--10 oz., thawed
        fresh strawberries--3 boxes
        orange liqueur--2 tablespoons
        powdered sugar--2 tablespoons

Mix raspberries in blender. Strain to remove seeds. Add
liqueur and sugar. Pour over berries. The sauce gives them
a beautiful glaze and preserves the strawberries as well.
May be prepared the day before serving. Serves 6.

*"Thy temples are like a pomegranate split open." (Song of
Songs)*

201

HOT FRUIT COMPOTE

A complement for a buffet dinner

apricot halves--29 oz. can
pear halves--29 oz. can
peach slices--29 oz. can
plums--29 oz. can, pitted
pitted sour cherries--16 oz. can
macaroons--12 large, crumbled
sliced almonds--4 oz.
butter--2 tablespoons
cinnamon--1 teaspoon, ground
brandy--1 tablespoon

Drain fruit and mix. Cover bottom of 9" casserole with 1/3 of the fruit. Cover with 1/3 of macaroons, almonds, butter, and cinnamon. Repeat 2 more times using up all ingredients. Bake at 350°F for 1 hour. Sprinkle with brandy. Serve warm.

Serves 12.

FAIRFAX FREEZE

A pretty and tasty dessert for chocolate lovers

unsweetened chocolate--4 oz. (4 squares)
butter--1 cup, softened
powdered sugar--2 cups
eggs--4 large
peppermint flavoring--1/4 teaspoon
vanilla--2 teaspoons
vanilla wafer crumbs--1 cup (approximately 26)
maraschino cherries--3 oz.
sweetened whipped cream--1/2 cup

Melt chocolate over hot water. In a mixer beat together butter and sugar until light and fluffy. Add chocolate and continue beating until smooth. Add eggs and blend well. Add peppermint and vanilla and beat until well blended. Place cup cake papers in muffin tins. Cover bottom of each cup with cookie crumbs. Spoon in mixture. Top with remaining crumbs and freeze. When ready to serve peel off paper and top with whipped cream and cherry. Makes 16 to 20.

203

DRIED FRUIT COMPOTE

        dried fruit--11 oz.
        water--1 cup
        brown sugar--1/4 cup
        butter--2 tablespoons
        salt--1/2 teaspoon
        sherry--1/4 cup
        pineapple tid-bits--8 oz. (fruit and juice)
        cinnamon--1 teaspoon
        raisins--1/2 cup
        bread crumbs--1/4 cup

Mix all ingredients together. Place into casserole dish.
Bake at 350°F for 1-1/2 hours.

MATZO AND APPLE PUDDING

A well received Passover pudding

        matzo farfel--3 cups (or broken matzo pieces)
        lemon juice--3 tablespoons
        lemon rind--1/4 teaspoon, grated
        eggs--2 large, slightly beaten
        salt--1/2 teaspoon
        chicken fat--2 teaspoons
        apples--4, peeled and sliced
        sugar--1/4 cup
        cinnamon--1 teaspoon
        white raisins--1/2 cup
        coconut--1/2 cup, shredded

Pour boiling water over matzo farfel to cover. Let sit 10
minutes. Pour off excess water pressing slightly with the
palm of your hand. Do not actually squeeze dry. Add lemon
juice, lemon rind, eggs, salt, and fat. Mix well. Cover
apples with sugar and cinnamon. Combine apples, matzo, and
raisins. Put into well buttered 9" pie tin. Cover with
coconut. Mix all ingredients together. Place into casserole
dish. Bake at 350°F for 1-1/2 hours. Serves 6.

FRESH PEACH DESSERT

        peaches--6
        honey--1/2 cup
        lemon juice--4 tablespoons
        butter--2 tablespoons
        cinnamon--1/2 teaspoon

Plunge peaches into hot water for 30 seconds. Loosen skins and remove. Split peaches in halves and remove pits. Place, cut side up, in a casserole dish.

Combine honey and lemon juice. Pour over peach halves. Dot with butter. Sprinkle with cinnamon. Bake at 350°F for 20 minutes.

FRIVOLOUS TRIFLE

Beautiful served in an over-sized brandy snifter

    vanilla pudding--3-1/4 oz. pkg. (not instant)
    milk--1-1/2 cups
    cream sherry--1/3 cup plus 2 tablespoons
    orange or pound cake--8 oz.
    strawberry jam--1 cup
    pears--2 lb. can, mashed (or 2 cups fresh strawberries)
    whipping cream--8 oz., whipped and sweetened

Cook pudding with milk and 1/3 cup sherry. Set aside.
Break cake into bite size pieces. Spread bottom of bowl
with 1/2 of the cake. Cover cake with 1 tablespoon cream
sherry, 1/2 of the fruit, and 1/2 of the jam. Make another
layer with the remaining cake and cover with another tablespoon of cream sherry, pears, and jam. Spread with warm
pudding. Set 4 hours. Cover with whipped cream. Serves 12.

STRAWBERRY CHEESE DELIGHT

A surprise package!

Crust:

flaked coconut--2 cups
sugar--2 tablespoons
flour--1 tablespoon
butter--2 tablespoons, melted

Filling:

strawberry preserves--10 oz.
cream cheese--8 oz., softened
powdered sugar--1/2 cup, sifted
chopped pecans--1/2 cup
almond extract--1 teaspoon
milk--1 tablespoon

Topping:

whipping cream--1 cup, whipped
powdered sugar--1/4 cup, sifted
pecans--8 halves

Combine coconut, sugar, flour, and butter. Press into bottom of a 9" greased spring form making a crust. Bake at 350°F for 10 minutes. Loosen crust from bottom of pan slightly to facilitate removal later. Chill.

Spread crust with 1/2 the strawberry preserves.

Combine cream cheese, 1/2 cup powdered sugar, pecans, and almond extract with the milk. Blend well and spread over layer of preserves.

Whip cream. Add 1/4 cup powdered sugar and continue whipping until stiff. Spoon over cheese layer. Garnish with remaining preserves and pecan halves. Freeze just until firm. Serves 10.

HELPFUL HINTS

When preparing hamburgers for the freezer, shape meat into a roll, cut in slices and insert waxed paper between each pattie.

Add a dash of dill weed or mild herb to scrambled eggs or broiled salmon.

from nibbles to noshes

HOLLANDAISE SAUCE

Try it - it's easy

```
butter--1/3 cup, not softened
lemon juice--1 tablespoon
red pepper--1/16 teaspoon
egg yolks--2 large, slightly beaten
```

Place all ingredients in small saucepan. Stab butter with a dinner fork. Stir constantly using piece of butter to mix with. Cook over very low heat. Beat with fork after butter melts. Keep beating and stirring until sauce begins to thicken. Remove from heat. Continue to stir until sauce coats fork. Immediately pour into serving dish. It will thicken slightly in dish.

Do not attempt to re-heat or keep warm. If sauce curdles, beat in a small amount of cream or put in blender.

TERIYAKI AMERICANO

We combined several recipes to make this one super-duper

        garlic--2 cloves, crushed
        soy sauce--1 cup
        green onions--3, chopped
        white onion--1 small, chopped
        brown sugar--4 tablespoons
        pineapple juice--4 tablespoons
        oil--2 tablespoons
        fresh ginger--1/4" piece, crushed
        white wine--2 tablespoons

Mix ingredients together. Use as a marinade on steaks or
hamburgers. Best for barbecued meats.

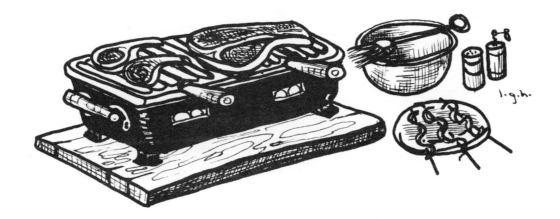

BRANDIED DATES

Send these to your family in the East

        fresh dates--2 lbs.
        brown sugar--1 cup
        water--1/2 cup
        brandy--1 cup

Cook sugar and water together until sugar melts. Add brandy.
Pour over dates. Seal tightly. Store for 3 weeks before
using.

CHOP SUEY STUFFING

A low calorie stuffing

margarine--1/2 cube
apples--2, peeled, sliced
onion--1 medium, sliced
celery--2 cups, chopped
cabbage--1 head, sliced
oranges--2 thick-skinned, unpeeled, sliced
ground ginger--1 teaspoon
soy sauce--1-1/2 tablespoons

Fry fruit and vegetables in margarine for 7 minutes. Stir
constantly. Add ginger and soy sauce. Cover and allow to
steam without heat for 5 minutes. Stuff turkey.

BUBBA'S STUFFING

Makes you think you're back at grandmother's house

margarine--1/2 cup
onion--1 medium, grated
egg bread--1 small loaf (leave crust on)
parsley--1/2 cup, chopped
eggs--4 large, beaten
salt--1/4 teaspoon
pepper--1/8 teaspoon

Melt margarine in a skillet. Add onion and saute until
golden yellow. Set aside.

Cover bread with water. Pour off water immediately and
squeeze dry. Add bread and parsley to onion. Cook until
bread is dry. Remove from heat. Cool. Add eggs, salt and
pepper. Mix well. Stuffs 2 large chickens or 1 turkey.

****

*"Cast thy bread upon the waters, for thou shalt find it
after many days." (Ecclesiastes)*

BEARNAISE SAUCE

Surprise your husband and serve it tonight

    hollandaise sauce--1 cup (8 oz. can)
    vermouth--1 tablespoon
    tarragon--1/2 teaspoon
    shallots--1 tablespoon, minced
    thyme--1/4 teaspoon

Mix all ingredients together.

OH JOY BARBECUE SAUCE

Great on beef ribs

    onion--1 small, minced
    green pepper--1 small, chopped fine
    oil--2 tablespoons
    brown sugar--2 tablespoons
    mustard--1 tablespoon, prepared
    Worcestershire sauce--1 tablespoon
    salt--1 teaspoon
    ketchup--3/4 cup

Mix all ingredients together. Put in pan and simmer over
slow heat for 15 minutes. Use as marinade on steaks, ribs,
or chicken.

PICK A PICKLE

So simple and so good

        salt--1/4 cup
        hot water--1 cup
        cold water--6 cups
        garlic bulbs--2, unpeeled, cut in small pieces
        pickling spices--1-1/4 oz. (1/2 pkg.)
        fresh dill--1 stalk
        pickling cucumbers--5 lbs., even size

Mix salt in hot water. Combine with cold water and set
aside.

In a 1 gallon container or crock, place garlic bulbs, pickling spices, and dill. Place cucumbers in the container in
an upright position tightly fitted. Fill container with the
water using additional cold water, if necessary, to fill to
top. If cucumbers do not fill container, place a plate on
top of them to keep them under the water. Put on cover and
place on kitchen counter out of sunlight for 48 to 72 hours.
Once each day, shake the container to mix the solution.

Then place container into refrigerator. Pickles are now
ready. As they remain in refrigerator, pickling process
will continue at a slow rate.

To use the solution a second time, add 1-1/4 oz. of pickling
spices (1/2 pkg.) and water, if necessary, and allow cucumbers to pickle 72 to 96 hours before refrigerating.

HOT RELISH PEARS

Very pretty on a dinner plate

Bartlett pear halves--29 oz. can, drained
celery--3 tablespoons, finely chopped
green pepper--3 tablespoons, finely chopped
pimiento--2 tablespoons, finely chopped
Italian salad dressing--4 tablespoons
salt--1/4 teaspoon
pepper--1/16 teaspoon

Combine celery, pepper, pimiento, 3 tablespoons salad dressing, salt, and pepper. Place pears cut side up in large
glass baking dish. Fill pears with relish mixture. Drizzle
pears with 1 tablespoon dressing. Bake at 350°F for 15
minutes.

STUFFED FRUIT

Just like the expensive kind

prunes--20 to 25 large
dried apricots--1 lb.
walnut halves--4 oz.
brandy--1/2 cup
corn syrup--1/4 cup

Steam the fruit until soft but not mushy. Do not soak or
boil. Pit the prunes. Put the apricots through the meat
chopper on coarse.

Mix the corn syrup and brandy together. Reserve 2 tablespoons. Combine remainder with the ground apricots.

Fill the prunes with the apricot mixture. Force 1 walnut
half into the middle of each stuffed prune. Fill fruit to
overflowing. Pour a drop of brandy syrup over each fruit.
Wrap in aluminum foil. Keep indefinitely without refriger-
ation.

*"Thy wife shall be as a fruitful vine, in the innermost
parts of thy house; thy children like olive plants, round
about thy table." (Psalms)*

EASY STRAWBERRY JAM

The only mistake with this recipe is not to try it

      ripe strawberries--2 pints
      sugar--4 cups
      lemon juice--2 tablespoons

Wash berries in cold water; just dip and drain. Hull them and put them into large sauce pan with 2 cups sugar. Bring to a boil and boil 2 minutes, stirring constantly. Add the remaining 2 cups of sugar and boil another 3 minutes. Continue to stir. Add lemon juice. Pour into 2 rimmed cookie sheets. Let stand overnight. Stir once in a while (if you are up).

In the morning you'll have homemade jam for your toast. Makes about 2 glasses.

ALMONDS

      almonds--2 lbs., shelled
      salt--1/8 teaspoon
      butter--2 tablespoons

Pour scalding water over nuts. Pinch off skins. Fry in the butter until lightly browned. Stir constantly. Spread on clean brown paper to cool. Salt and serve.

MARMALADE

Easier, cheaper, and better than store bought

    grapefruit--1 large
    navel oranges--6 to 10 depending on size
    sugar--6 to 8 cups
    Sur-jel--1 pkg.

First day - thinly slice fruit to make 9 cups firmly packed. Place in large stainless steel or enamel pot. Add 12 cups water. Cover and set overnight.

Second day - boil mixture down 30 minutes or until about 3/4 of original.

Third day - add 1 cup of sugar for each cup of fruit plus juice. Cook 1-1/2 to 2 hours or until mixture boils down 25%. Add 1 package Sur-jel. Allow to set overnight to be sure mixture has thickened well. Place in glass jars and seal.

Makes 6 to 7 pints.

CINNAMON WALNUTS

An excellent bread and butter gift

    sugar--1 cup
    evaporated milk--1/3 cup
    cinnamon--1 teaspoon
    salt--1/4 teaspoon
    vanilla--1/4 teaspoon
    walnuts--2 cups, halves

Mix sugar, milk, cinnamon, and salt in a 4 quart pot. Stir over heat until dissolved. Boil to 238°F (medium soft ball). Stir occasionally to prevent burning. Add vanilla; then nuts. Mix well, being sure all nuts are covered. Spread out individually on wax paper to dry. These are so delicious that I didn't serve them to the company. I kept them for my husband.

"Come ye, buy and eat: Yea, come, buy wine and milk" (Isaiah)

RUM BALLS

A prize winner - cheap to make but expensive to buy

        cocoa--1/2 cup
        powdered sugar--1-1/2 cups
        chopped walnuts--1 cup
        sweetened condensed milk--1/2 cup
        good rum (no substitute)--1-1/2 teaspoons

    Frosting:

        cocoa--2 tablespoons
        powdered sugar--2 tablespoons

Mix cocoa and powdered sugar thoroughly. Add nuts, milk,
and rum. Combine ingredients well. Form into 1" balls.
Let balls stand while mixing the last 2 ingredients. Roll
balls in this mixture. Yield about 2 dozen. Keep refriger-
ated.

CHOCOLATE PEANUT CLUSTERS

Make your own candy - easy

        semi-sweet chocolate chips--12 oz.
        salted peanuts--2 cups, shelled and skinned
        dark raisins--2 cups

Melt chocolate chips in double boiler. Cool. Add raisins
and nuts. Other nuts may be substituted.

Drop from a teaspoon onto a piece of waxed paper or onto a
marble slab. Allow to cool. Yields about 80 pieces.

****

"Flee away into the land of Judah and there eat bread" (Amos)

"Eat and drink sayeth he to thee." (Proverbs)

"For the churning of milk bringeth forth curd." (Proverbs)

SANGRIA

A South American fresher upper

    burgundy wine--1 fifth of a gallon
    orange juice--1-1/2 cups
    lemon juice--1/4 cup
    sugar--1/8 cup
    orange liqueur--1 tablespoon
    brandy--2 tablespoons
    club soda--6 oz.
    orange--1/2, thinly sliced
    lemon--1/4, thinly sliced
    apple--1/2, thinly sliced

Mix wine, orange juice, lemon juice, sugar, orange liqueur,
and brandy. Chill. Fill water pitcher that has an ice trap
with ice. Pour in wine. Add sliced fruit and chilled soda
water just before serving.

Serves 6.

PINK LADY COOLER

        instant tea mix--1.8 oz. pkg.
        frozen pink lemonade--6 oz. can
        water--1-1/2 quarts
        ice cubes

Mix instant tea, water, and pink lemonade. Pour over ice
cubes before serving. Serves 5.

ANOTHER PINK LADY

        frozen punch concentrate--6 oz. can
        frozen pink lemonade--6 oz. can
        water--1-1/2 quarts
        ice cubes
        raspberry sherbet--1 pint

Mix punch, lemonade, and water. Add ice cubes and sherbet
just before serving. Serves 5.

CHI-CHI

        vodka--6 oz.
        lemon juice--2 tablespoons
        pineapple juice--8 oz.
        coconut syrup--4 oz.
        pineapple chunks--4
        maraschino cherries--4

Pour all liquids in blender and mix well. Put crushed ice
in 12 oz. glass. Pour liquid in glass. Place a pineapple
chunk and a cherry on a toothpick and place on top of drink.

Serves 4.

HELPFUL HINTS

When preparing broiled grapefruit, pour either a little green creme
de menthe or rum over top before broiling.

To remove excess fat from soup, wrap an ice cube in cheese cloth and
skim over top. Fat will congeal on cube.

INDEX

Title	Page

****

Additional copies of this book may be purchased from the
Beverly Hills Chapter of Hadassah
8827 W. Olympic Blvd.
Beverly Hills, Calif. 90211
(213) 652-5601

HADASSAH, the Women's Zionist Organization of America, Inc.
Proceeds to support its program in Israel & the U.S.A.